Practical Astrology

THE EASY WAY

This book is dedicated to my friends Roy and Elaine Noble

and all the crew at BBC Radio Wales.

Practical Astrology

THE EASY WAY

Creative director: Sarah King
Editor: Judith Millidge
Project editor: Yvonne Worth
Designer: 2H Design

Library of Congress Cataloging-in-Publication Data Available

10   9   8   7   6   5   4   3   2   1

Published in 2003 by Sterling Publishing Company, Inc.
387 Park Avenue South, New York, N.Y. 10016

This book was designed and produced by
D&S Books Ltd
Kerswell, Parkham Ash
Bideford, Devon, EX39 5PR

© 2003 D&S Books

Distributed in Canada by Sterling Publishing
c/o Canadian Manda Group,
One Atlantic Avenue, Suite 105
Toronto, Ontario, Canada M6K 3E7

Every effort has been made to ensure that all the information in this book is accurate. however, due to differing conditions, tools, and individual skills, the publisher cannot be responsible for any injuries, losses, and other damages which may result from the use of the information in this book.

Printed in China

Sterling ISBN 1-4027-0586-7

Contents

Introduction
EASY ASTROLOGY?

There are only two simple calculations to be made. This diagram will help you find your rising sign.

There's no denying that astrology is a difficult business—there is much more to it than simply reading your horoscope in the daily paper. I almost gave up before I had begun because of the endless tables and mathematical formulae that had to be studied long before getting to the interesting bit of actually interpreting a birth chart. Which, I might add, is what I wanted to do in the first place. I eventually plucked up the courage to persevere and soon became pretty good at the calculation part, finding that balancing the interpretations was actually the most difficult bit. Be that as it may, it is clear that although many people are interested in the subject, it is the vexed question of the calculations that tends to put them off. This book is the answer to the problem!

Practical Astrology the Easy Way is exactly what it says. Most of the information that you will need, to set up a reasonably accurate birth chart, is listed here, with all the hard work completed. There are only two simple calculations to be made in the entire book, namely "Finding your Moon sign" and "Finding your rising sign." All the rest is a matter of looking up the relevant information, and writing it down on your blank chart, which you will find on p.29. If you don't want to spoil your book, or are afraid of making a mistake, simply photocopy the page.

As you progress through the book you will see how easy it is. I've abandoned most of the complicated stuff like degrees (360 in a circle), precise aspects (angles between planets) and decans (thirds of a star sign), and wherever complexity threatened to creep in, I've consistently chosen the simplest way of getting a result.

You won't need to do much counting—all the difficult calculations have been done for you.

The rules

So, for the purposes of this book, the houses of the horoscope (p.23) occupy a whole zodiac sign. All planets within a zodiac sign are considered to be in conjunction, all planets in opposite signs are considered to be in opposition (see Planetary aspects p.124), and so on for all the other aspects.

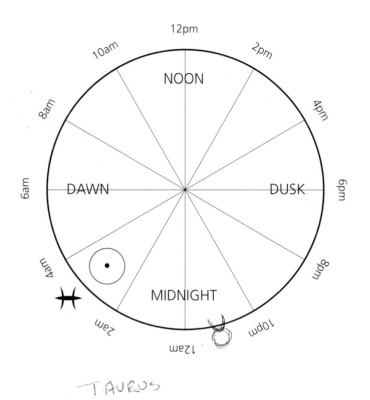

TAURUS

Step 1

The first task is to find your Sun sign (p.12) and mark it on the blank birth chart (Step 1). Most people already know their Sun sign, so this is the easiest part.

Step 2

The next part (Step 2) is slightly more complicated, because you have to find the Moon sign and the rising sign. Full instructions for these calculations are given on pp.26–28. These points must also be marked on your blank birth chart.

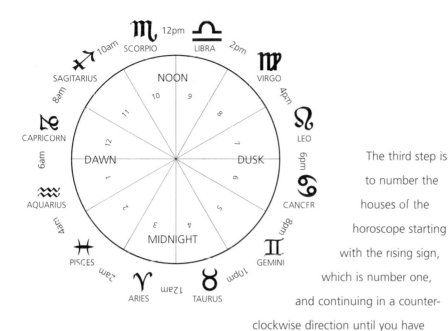

The third step is to number the houses of the horoscope starting with the rising sign, which is number one, and continuing in a counter-clockwise direction until you have numbered all twelve (Step 3). So, if you find that your rising sign is in Gemini, then Cancer will be house two, Leo will be house four, and so on, until you reach Taurus, which will be house twelve. The houses are almost as important (some would say equally as important) as the signs of the zodiac themselves.

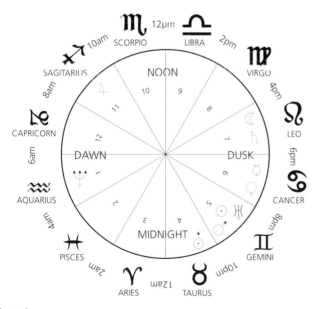

Step 4

The fourth step is to look up each of the planets and add them to the appropriate place on your blank birth chart. This will give you your own unique horoscope (the word horoscope has nothing to do with 'star sign' columns in magazines—it actually means "the map of the hour" in Greek).

Don't confuse your own unique horoscope (birth chart) with the columns that appears in newspapers and magazines.

You should now have a complete birth chart. The Sun, the Moon, and each of the planets will be placed in a sign of the zodiac and in a house of the horoscope. So, the Sun might be in Leo in the seventh house, the Moon might be in Cancer in the sixth house, and so on for all the planets.

The signs of the zodiac and the houses have a great deal in common with each other, so I have combined the interpretations of the signs and the houses. Throughout the book you will find entries such as "Moon in Aries or the first house," or "Mars in Gemini or the third house." This means that if the Moon happens to be in Aries you would read that entry, but if the Moon also happens to be in the seventh house you would also read "Moon in Libra or the seventh house," and combine the two interpretations. The same applies to the Sun and all the other planets.

The circle of stars

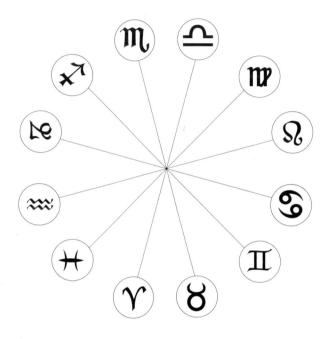

Anyone familiar with magazine horoscope columns might be forgiven for thinking that the zodiac of the twelve signs is a list. However, it should not be forgotten that the zodiac is actually a circle. It is an imaginary band encircling the earth following the paths of the Sun, Moon, and planets. From ancient times, this band has been divided into twelve segments, which are the familiar signs of the zodiac. When each segment was originally conceived, their names were taken from the starry constellation that occupied that segment. The slightly uneven rotation of the Earth on its axis has meant that, over time, the zodiacal constellations have "slipped" and no longer occupy exactly the segments with which they share a name. So, the name Aries the Ram is applied not just to a pattern of stars but also to a segment of the sky called a zodiac sign. In other words, a constellation and a star sign are not the same thing.

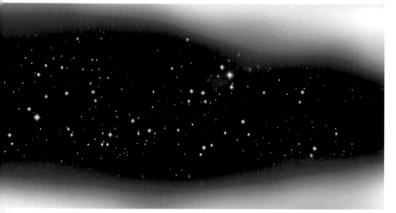

The word zodiac literally means "circle of animals" even though there are human and semi-human figures included, in addition to a pair of scales. Tradition has ascribed a set of characteristics to each of the zodiac signs and these are covered in more depth in "Your Sun Sign" p.11–22.

A word to the wise

Remember that this book will give you a reasonably accurate, personalized birth chart. Most of the information given is completely precise, but there is a margin for error in the calculations of the Moon sign and the rising sign, a well as an assumption made in the case of the position of the planet Mercury. If, after reading the relevant entries for the Moon, Mercury, and the rising sign, you feel that it just isn't you,

then look at the interpretations of the signs on either side of it. If one of these fits better, then it is extremely probable that this is the one for you. All the other solar and planetary positions should be completely accurate.

Enjoy your first foray into the wonderful world of astrology.

Your Sun Sign

The Sun is our parent star. The sun is the origin of the planets and, indeed, the source of life itself. Consequently, this massive fiery orb dominates the art of astrology. All the planetary bodies, including our Earth, orbit around it in a majestic clockwork of time and space. The Sun, therefore, seems to move through each of the twelve signs of the zodiac in an endless sequence.

The vast majority of people know their Sun sign, although, inaccurately, they will tend to call it their "star sign." Identifying the Sun sign is the easiest part of easy astrology. Here is a list, complete with dates, to help you find anyone's Sun sign.

Aries the Ram

March 21–April 19

Leo the Lion

July 23– August 22

Sagittarius the Archer

November 22–December 21

Taurus the Bull

April 20–May 20

Virgo the Virgin

August 23–September 22

Capricorn the Goat

December 22–January 19

Gemini the Twins

May 21–June 21

Libra the Scales

September 23–October 23

Aquarius the Water Carrier

January 20–February 18

Cancer the Crab

June 22–July 22

Scorpio the Scorpion

October 24–November 21

Pisces the Fish

February 19–March 20

Aries is considered to be the first sign of the zodiac, because it starts at the spring equinox (when day and night are of equal length). This point used to be considered the beginning of the new year long before it was decided to move it to January 1.

Some people who were born around a sign changeover say that they "were born on the cusp" and think that they therefore belong to two Sun signs. This is not the case. They will invariably display characteristics of one sign or the other and must therefore be considered to have been "born under" the sign that has most affinity with them.

When you ask someone what sign they were born under, it is their Sun sign that you are inquiring after, because this is the sign that the Sun appeared to be traveling through at their time of birth. Regardless of anything else that might be on a person's birth chart, the Sun sign is a pretty powerful indicator of a person's character. The Sun sign alone is often enough to show you whether you want to get to know a person better or not. An easy way to categorize people is by the gender, element, and quality of their Sun sign, so let us look at these now.

Categories

Each sign belongs to a *gender*, either masculine or feminine; each is assigned an *element* of fire, earth, air, or water; and each belongs to a *quality* of cardinal, fixed, or mutable. There are six signs of each gender, three of each element, and four of each quality. This means that each sign is different, although they may share some common ground with several others. This is how the system works.

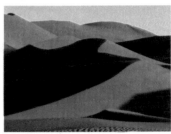

Above left: The signs of the zodiac are classified by their respective "elements"—fire, air, earth, and water.

Sign categories

Sign	Gender	Element	Quality
Aries	Masculine	Fire	Cardinal
Taurus	Feminine	Earth	Fixed
Gemini	Masculine	Air	Mutable
Cancer	Feminine	Water	Cardinal
Leo	Masculine	Fire	Fixed
Virgo	Feminine	Earth	Mutable
Libra	Masculine	Air	Cardinal
Scorpio	Feminine	Water	Fixed
Sagittarius	Masculine	Fire	Mutable
Capricorn	Feminine	Earth	Cardinal
Aquarius	Masculine	Air	Fixed
Pisces	Feminine	Water	Mutable

The genders

The terms *masculine* and *feminine* have nothing to do with sexuality as such. Masculine signs are more positive, assertive, and outgoing, while feminine ones are more receptive, nurturing, and long-suffering.

The elements

The elements relate to the ancient beliefs that air, earth, fire, and water were pure, indivisible substances from which everything in the universe was constructed in differing degrees. Each element is believed to convey certain characteristics. (NB: beginners to astrology often think that Aquarius is a water sign because its symbol is that of the water carrier, but it is actually an *air* sign.)

THE FIRE GROUP

Masculine *Aries, Leo, Sagittarius*

If you belong to a fire sign, you will think and act quickly, and you will be quick to take up opportunities when they come along. You have some powerful leadership qualities. You can be a little selfish at times, simply because you don't always stop to look at the way your actions impinge on those who are around you. However, your heart is in the right place and you are idealistic, spontaneous, loving, and generous. You are less confident than you appear, and you can become depressed when too much goes wrong.

THE EARTH GROUP

Feminine *Taurus, Virgo, Capricorn*

You are practical, sensible, and hard-working, and you can be relied upon to do what is asked of you. You may not rush at anything, because you prefer to work at your own pace. Security is important to you, both in a financial sense and also in your personal relationships. You are shrewd in business and perhaps a little too materialistic, but at least you are prepared to provide for yourself and your family.

THE AIR GROUP

Masculine   Gemini, Libra, Aquarius

Yours is a sociable group and you like to be up-to-date. Even if you are not out partying all the time, you need to keep in touch with others and to know what is going on in your environment. In business, you prefer to meet people face-to-face and to communicate in a clear and open manner. You are not particularly clever with money, but you work hard and generally stay out of debt. Tension and worry get you down. Being a little detached, you can't cope with a partner who is too clinging and emotionally dependent.

THE WATER GROUP

Feminine   Cancer, Scorpio, Pisces

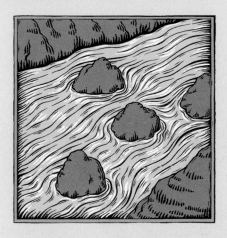

You may appear slow on the uptake, because you need time to think about things before committing yourself, but your intuition is strong and you can rely upon it to guide you. Your shrewdness and insight can make you a successful business person. Your emotions and feelings are profound and you can be badly hurt. You love deeply and you rarely let down your devoted friends, loved ones, or children.

The qualities

The three qualities reflect quality of life, and each of the four zodiac signs within each of the qualities represents a different element.

THE CARDINAL GROUP

Aries, Cancer, Libra, Capricorn

If you belong to a cardinal sign, you have far more determination than others realize. You take care to get the best for yourself, your family, and for anybody else for whom you feel responsible. When you need to fight for something, you display great strength.

THE FIXED GROUP

Taurus, Leo, Scorpio, Aquarius

You can initiate action, but your main talent is keeping going and seeing things through. You prefer to maintain the status quo and to avoid taking unnecessary risks. Both financial and emotional support is a necessity for you, and you also try to provide this for those who you love. Your chief fault is obstinacy, and either furious anger or deep depression when things go wrong.

THE MUTABLE GROUP

Gemini, Virgo, Sagittarius, Pisces

You need variety and you can cope with fluctuating and changeable circumstances better than most. You prefer a job that takes you from place to place, or where you deal with new people on a daily basis. You may choose an unconventional lifestyle that suits your spiritual or emotional requirements. Some of you manage all this while also keeping a home and a settled relationship going, others move around or even drift. You long for success, achievement, and even fame but you may lack the drive or the confidence that is needed to achieve this.

Characteristics of the individual Sun signs

 ### ARIES THE RAM

Hot-headed Aries is the pioneer of the zodiac, with a youthful exuberance that will never be lost. He not only likes, but needs, a challenge in his life, and can be quite forceful in achieving his aims. Sun in Aries people are spontaneous, stimulating, energetic and direct. To Ariens, actions speak louder than words! They like an uncomplicated life, and want others to act in a straightforward manner too. When thwarted, the Aries temper can be awesome, but seldom lasts long.

March 21–April 19
Element: fire
Gender: masculine
Quality: cardinal
Ruler: Mars
Motto: I do!
Similar to: 1st house

Aries people are energetic, direct, and often selfish.

TAURUS THE BULL

Security, both emotional and financial, is of paramount importance to a person with the Sun in Taurus. In a positive sense this gives a protective personality with a strong sense of practicality and fairness. In a more negative sense, a Taurean may become possessive, possibly too careful with money, and jealous of others. Sharing often becomes an issue with this type. This person is persistent, has great powers of endurance, is usually trustworthy, and loves luxury.

20 April–20 May
Element: earth
Gender: feminine
Quality: fixed
Ruler: Venus
Motto: I own!
Similar to: 2nd house

Taureans are often money minded and need security.

♊ GEMINI THE TWINS

The dual nature of Gemini makes any summation of the sign difficult. It is true that Geminians are adaptable, extremely versatile, usually talkative, and amusing company. They love variety and are witty, spontaneous people. However, they can be regarded as fickle, too changeable, and unable to control their nervous energy. The Gemini curiosity is proverbial, as is the Geminian ability to see all arguments from both sides, often at once. This is a complex individual.

Witty, amusing Geminis are never boring company.

May 21–June 21
Element: air
Gender: masculine
Quality: mutable
Ruler: Mercury
Motto: I communicate!
Similar to: 3rd house

♋ CANCER THE CRAB

The charitable impulses of Cancer the Crab are not to be underestimated. They are thought of as being tough on the outside and soft in the middle, and it is true that they are sensitive (sometimes far too sensitive). This individual has strong instincts and is extremely protective of loved ones. Tenacious, shrewd, cautious, and thrifty, Cancerians regard the home and family as their ultimate concern. On the negative side, a Cancerian can be very moody and susceptible to flattery.

The maternal instincts of Cancerians ensure that they are very protective of loved ones.

June 22–July 22
Element: water
Gender: feminine
Quality: cardinal
Ruler: Moon
Motto: I nurture!
Similar to: 4th house

♌ LEO THE LION

Generosity is the hallmark of the dramatic Leo personality. This is the monarch of the zodiac and he won't let you forget it! However, Leos are magnanimous to those less fortunate than themselves. They are broadminded, great organizers, and are masters of dramatic flourishes that are the soul of showmanship. The more negative Leo might be a bit of a bully, fixed in opinions, and irritatingly patronizing. It goes without saying that a Leo is always right—the problem is that they often are!

July 23–August 22
Element: fire
Gender: masculine
Quality: fixed
Ruler: Sun
Motto: I rule!
Similar to: 5th house

Leos are masters of dramatic gestures and are very generous.

♍ VIRGO THE VIRGIN

Clever Virgos are the martyrs of the zodiac, ready to put themselves out for anyone. Caring, meticulous, and modest, this analytical, meticulous type often forgets his own interests while looking after the welfare of others. This is a person with an eye for detail. The Virgo may be a critic, sometimes hyper-critical, yet the process is usually an internal one, because no one could nit-pick at a Virgo more than the Virgo in question. Virgo is a worrier, possibly too fussy, and usually too concerned about what other people think.

August 23–September 22
Element: earth
Gender: feminine
Quality: mutable
Ruler: Mercury
Motto: I serve!
Similar to: 6th house

Virgos tend to be intelligent but can be prone to needless anxieties.

LIBRA THE SCALES

Charming, diplomatic Librans need harmony in their lives if they are to be truly happy. These people hate confrontation, sour atmospheres, and making snap judgments. Careful decision-making provides a major trait because, if the truth be told, Librans hate making decisions at all. Very relationship orientated, Librans are true romantics. They are refined, idealistic, and generally easy-going. However, they might be too frivolous and much too easily influenced by others, being ready to fall in love at the drop of a hat.

September 23–October 23
Element: air
Gender: masculine
Quality: cardinal
Ruler: Venus
Motto: I co-operate
Similar to: 7th house

Partnership and romance are very important to the Libran self-image.

SCORPIO THE SCORPION

Scorpio generally gets a bad press, the "sting in the tail" being the comment most usually associated with this sign. But there is another side: Scorpios have deep emotions and a powerfully determined sense of purpose. There is a magnetic intensity about them that is very attractive. They are also highly imaginative, with subtle perception and powerful insight combined with innate discretion (some would say secretiveness). On the other hand, the "sting" might have some foundation in a tendency to be unforgiving and possibly vengeful.

October 24–November 21
Element: water
Gender: feminine
Quality: fixed
Rulers: Mars and Pluto
Motto: I investigate
Similar to: 8th house

Scorpios are usually more determined to get things done than anyone else.

SAGITTARIUS THE ARCHER

November 22–December 21
Element: fire
Gender: masculine
Quality: mutable
Ruler: Jupiter
Motto: I'm free!
Similar to: 9th house

The versatile sign of Sagittarius ensures that those born under the influence of the Archer are open-minded, generally optimistic, exuberant, and freedom-loving. Truth and openness are very important to these types, and these are the characteristics that they both express and look for in others. The main fault of these individuals is that they can get carried away with their own enthusiasm. They may be too outspoken and rather tactless, or too restless and blindly optimistic. Generally, Sagittarians are usually very lucky individuals.

Sagittarians are exuberant and fun-loving.

CAPRICORN THE GOAT

December 22–January 19
Element: earth
Gender: feminine
Quality: cardinal
Ruler: Saturn
Motto: I aspire!
Similar to: 10th house

Ambition and status are close to the Capricorn heart, and it is a rare Goat who leaves this world in a poorer state than when he entered it. People of this sign are reliable, prudent, determined, and cautious, with a powerful sense of duty and discipline. Patient and persevering, Capricorns will climb the ladder of success, very rarely putting a foot wrong. On the more negative side, Capricorns can be inclined to pessimism, fixed in their views, and may be miserly with their cash.

Capricorns are ambitious but may be too cautious and pessimistic.

♒ AQUARIUS THE WATER CARRIER

Independence is the watchword for Aquarius, because those born under this sign hate to be restricted in any way. They know that the future will be far more interesting than the past, they are progressive, often revolutionary in thinking, humanitarian, idealistic, inventive, and friendly. They are lovers of humanity as a whole, although they may have some trouble with individuals. On the other hand, Aquarians can be unpredictable, eccentric, and rebelious for no reason. Many Aquarians strive to be unconventional—this is certainly not a boring sign.

January 20–February 18
Element: air
Gender: masculine
Quality: fixed
Ruler: Uranus
Motto: I originate!
Similar to: 11th house

Inventive Aquarians have a reputation for eccentricity.

♓ PISCES THE FISH

It is said that the two fish swim in opposite directions, and this trait is evident in many Pisceans. This is a very emotional sign with easily stirred sympathies, and a deeply compassionate nature. Of course this great heart cannot encompass all causes, even though the inclination to do so is strong, and Pisceans often feel at odd with themselves. Pisceans possess a strong intuition and many have psychic qualities. However, they may also be vague, careless, and easily confused by the conflicting views of others.

February 19–March 20
Element: water
Gender: feminine
Quality: mutable
Ruler: Neptune
Motto: I dream
Similar to: 12th house

Pisceans are intuitive and possess deep empathy with others.

As well as providing a reading for the Sun signs, we will be returning to this list of characteristics when we look at the interpretation of the rising sign.

FINDING YOUR RISING SIGN AND THE HOUSES OF THE HOROSCOPE

Your Sun sign is one of the twelve signs of the zodiac, and the particular one you belong to is dependent on your date of birth. The rising sign (astrologers call this the "ascendant") is based on the time of day that you were born.

Many people have no idea at all at what hour they first entered the world. If this is the case then you will have to ignore the rising sign and the system of astrological houses completely, although this does not mean that you cannot have a horoscope chart, it's just that some pieces of information will be missing. So if you don't know your time of birth, then skip this section and go on to "Finding your Moon Sign" on pp.57–62.

For those who do have an idea of when they were born (even if it's only a vague time), the rising sign provides some valuable extra information. This is because the rising sign modifies the characteristics of your Sun sign. So, when you have worked out your personal rising sign, read the section that follows to see how it adjusts the reading of your essential character.

The exact time of birth is an important factor in astrology.

The horoscope is the map of the sky at the time of birth.

What is the rising sign?

The rising sign is the sign that happens to be rising on the eastern horizon at the time of your birth. If you were born at dawn then it is likely that the rising sign and the Sun sign are exactly the same. When this occurs, people born with this combined influence are usually extremely typical of their sign. Most others will find that their rising sign and Sun sign are different, so it is possible that a person could be Virgo with Cancer rising or a Capricorn with Aries rising and so on. In most cases the rising sign reveals how a person would like the world to see him or her. It is the outer image, as opposed to the Sun sign which reveals the essential character. In astrological terms, the rising sign is of equal importance to the Sun sign (pp.11–22) and the Moon sign (pp.57–68).

Finding the rising sign is also useful when assessing astrological forecasts. Everybody is used to reading their horoscopes in magazines and newspapers and this activity can be made more personal and accurate if you read your rising sign forecast as well and combine the two.

This method of finding the rising sign without wrestling with any complicated sums works about 80 percent of the time. If you want to be completely sure about your rising sign then you really should consult a competent astrologer or invest in an astrological computer program. Having said that, this system does work with reasonable accuracy, although to be completely sure you should read the interpretations of the rising signs on either side of the one you have worked out. So, if your Sun sign happens to be Aries, and you work out that your rising sign is Leo, then you should also look at Cancer (the sign before Leo), and Virgo (the sign after Leo), to minimize any possible errors.

Newspaper "horoscope" columns can be made more accurate if you take the rising sign into account.

How to find your rising sign

Look at Figure 1, below. You will notice that it has the time of day around the edge of the circle rather like a clock face, with the hours arranged in two hour blocks and dawn and dusk marked across the horizontal axis.

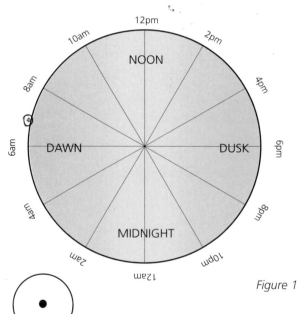

Figure 1

Place the symbol representing the Sun (a circle with a dot in the middle) in the segment that corresponds to your time of birth (do this even if you only know the approximate time). If you were born in Daylight Saving Time remember to deduct one hour from your birth time.

This is the symbol for the sun. It should be drawn on the diagram at your time of birth.

You already know your Sun sign (this is the sign that the Sun occupied on your date of birth). Place the name of that sign (or its symbol if you are feeling confident—see the key on pp.17–22) outside the circle near to your Sun symbol and time of birth as in Figure 2 (right). This shows a person who was born between 2am and 4am under the sign of Pisces.

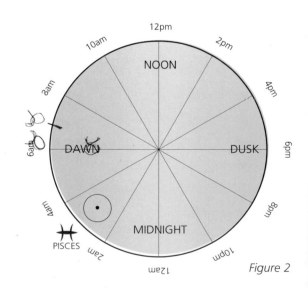

Figure 2

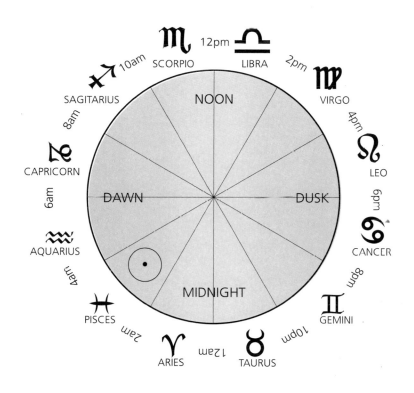

Now all the other star signs are added in a counter-clockwise direction.

EXAMPLE

This example is to show what to do if you have an awkward time of birth, in this case 10am. This places the Sun symbol directly on the 10am line between two blocks of time. The Sun sign is Capricorn, so the name (or symbol) for Capricorn goes outside the circle directly above the Sun symbol.

The sign on the left-hand side of the chart at the dawn point is Pisces so this is a person with the Sun sign of Capricorn with Pisces rising.

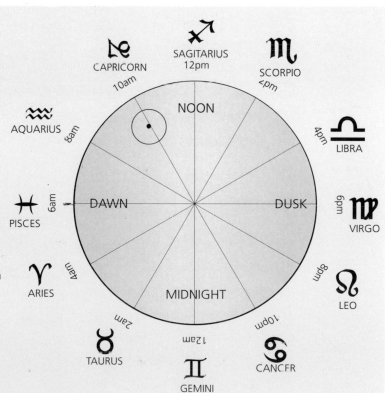

Now it's your turn! The figure opposite is a blank clockface. All you have to do is draw the Sun symbol at your time of birth (for a Daylight Saving Time birth remember to deduct one hour).

Now add your birth sign symbol outside the circle directly adjacent to the Sun symbol.

Fill in the other signs of the zodiac in their correct order in a counter-clockwise direction.

The sign on the left-hand side (dawn point) is most likely your rising sign (it will be in more than 80 percent of cases), but, to be completely sure, read the signs on either side to see if they fit the outward expression of your personality better.

Your rising sign is . . .

Now you can mark this sign on your personal horoscope chart by writing "rising sign" next to it.

To find out what your rising sign means to you turn to "Your Sun Sign" on pp.17–22 and read the relevant entry remembering that, this time, the interpretation is about the outer expression of your personality rather than your inner characteristics.

The ruler of your chart

The planet that rules your rising sign will also rule your entire birth chart. This planet is therefore a very important influence in your life. Once you have found your rising sign, the information given on pp.17–22 will reveal your chart ruler.

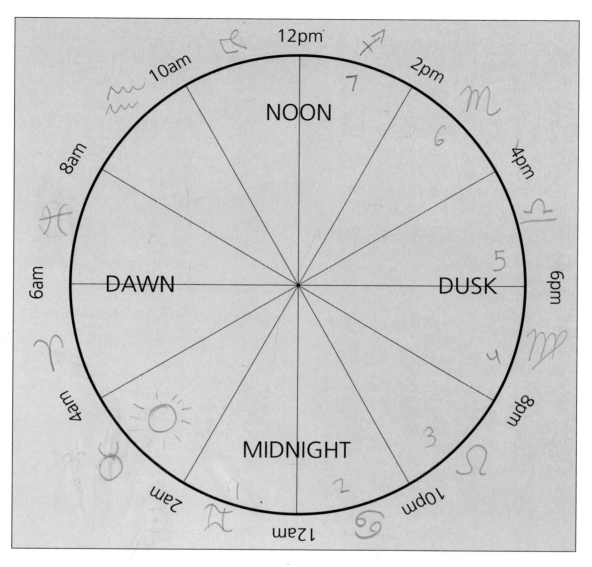

Your rising sign is _____ Gemini _____

The sun is in _____ Aries /Taurus _____ in the _____ house

The moon is in _____ Sagittarius _____ in the _____ house

Mercury is in _____ Pisces? _____ in the _____ house

Venus is in _____ in the _____ house

Mars is in _____ in the _____ house

Jupiter is in _____ in the _____ house

Saturn is in _____ in the _____ house

Uranus is in _____ in the _____ house

Neptune is in _____ in the _____ house

Pluto is in _____ in the _____ house

How the rising sign modifies your Sun sign

This section offers a brief guide as to how the mixture of Sun signs and rising signs will affect you.

ARIES WITH ARIES RISING

All the Arien traits are strongly marked. If you were born before dawn, you are very outgoing and adventurous but, if you were born after the Sun had risen, you will be much quieter, artistic, and drawn to mystical or psychic matters.

ARIES WITH TAURUS RISING

Your outer manner is fairly quiet and shy, and you may be a keen musician, cook, or gardener. You are more settled and less adventurous than other Arians.

ARIES WITH GEMINI RISING

You are clever and quick thinking and you can do a dozen things at once. Your moods are mercurial and you change your mind quickly.

ARIES WITH CANCER RISING

You are close to your family, very home loving, and also very careful with money. Interested in military matters, you may be attracted to teaching or helping the needy.

ARIES WITH LEO RISING

You may be bumptious and aggravating at times, but you are great fun and a very loving and affectionate partner. You may love travel and education.

Aries people who have Aries rising can be attracted to mysticism.

ARIES WITH VIRGO RISING

You are quieter, more modest, and more hard-working than most Ariens. You lack confidence, but you are ambitious and keen on healing, psychic, or investigative matters.

ARIES WITH LIBRA RISING

You are much more laid back than the average Arien and you wait for other people to motivate you. You are good looking with a sexy, charismatic personality.

Aries people who have Pisces rising are often drawn to a sporting way of life.

ARIES WITH SCORPIO RISING

You have a powerhouse personality, being a really hard worker and go-getter who won't let anything stand in your way. You could be very interest in the military, police, or engineering work.

ARIES WITH SAGITTARIUS RISING

You are a true pioneer, an adventurer with very itchy feet. You could take up a very glamorous job or become something wonderful like being a comedian or a top ballet dancer.

ARIES WITH CAPRICORN RISING

You are a very powerful personality who wants to reach the top and this may compensate you for a difficult childhood.

ARIES WITH AQUARIUS RISING

You have an unusual attitude toward money and goods, possibly amassing them and then giving them away again. You value education and you have a clever, inventive mind.

ARIES WITH PISCES RISING

You may be quiet, shy and nondescript, but you have a powerfully self-centred ambition. You could choose an artistic, sporting or glamorous way of life.

Those Ariens with Virgo rising are often interesting in healing.

TAURUS WITH LEO RISING

You are determined to make a success of your life and career, and you may be drawn to the theater, music, or some other kind of glamorous job.

TAURUS WITH VIRGO RISING

You have an eye for detail and you could be an artistic craftsman. Your outer manner is quiet and reserved and you don't like making a fool of yourself.

TAURUS WITH LIBRA RISING

You love beauty in all its forms, and you could be an excellent gardener. You are reasonably confident, as long as you are dealing with things that you know about.

TAURUS WITH ARIES RISING

You are a real go-getter who won't let much stand in your way. You could be attracted to work in the armed services or in a large and well-structured organization

TAURUS WITH TAURUS RISING

This is Taurus in its purest form, and all the Taurean traits are strongly marked. If you were born before dawn, you are more outgoing; if after dawn, quieter and more reserved.

TAURUS WITH GEMINI RISING

There is a spiritual side to you, which means that you must do something that you believe in. You are more talkative and outgoing than most Taureans.

TAURUS WITH CANCER RISING

You are very close to your family, and your home means a lot to you. You could collect valuable, beautiful, or antique items, and you love music.

A Taurean with Cancer rising is often musically gifted.

TAURUS WITH SCORPIO RISING

You try to cooperate with others and to live a peaceful life, but you are prepared to fight for the things that you consider important.

TAURUS WITH SAGITTARIUS RISING

You are far more outgoing and talkative than the average Taurean and you need a good deal of personal freedom. You enjoy travel and you may work in the tourist or communications industries.

TAURUS WITH CAPRICORN RISING

You need material security, but you also have strong spiritual values. You need to work in an area which helps humanity or that is important to you.

TAURUS WITH AQUARIUS RISING

Sometimes you are sensible, money-minded, and in need of security, and, at other times, you throw caution to the wind and take off in strange directions. You can be very stubborn and determined.

A Taurus with Capricorn rising wants to help humanity.

TAURUS WITH PISCES RISING

You could be very artistic and musical, and you must be surrounded by beautiful things. Your values are spiritual rather than material.

The Taurean sense of values is directed to the spiritual when Pisces is rising.

GEMINI WITH ARIES RISING

With an outgoing personality you have the ability to inspire others, but you may not be too gentle with their feelings.

GEMINI WITH TAURUS RISING

You may have a real head for figures, choosing to work as an accountant or a banker. You are keen on art, music, and craftwork.

GEMINI WITH GEMINI RISING

Your childhood difficulties take a long time to shake off and you may have to wait until middle age to reach your potential. If you were born before dawn, you will have more confidence than if you were born after dawn.

GEMINI WITH CANCER RISING

You are quieter and more gentle than the average Gemini and you are probably drawn to work in one of the caring professions, although you value money too.

GEMINI WITH LEO RISING

You need a good standard of living and you probably work hard to create this. You get on well with all kinds of people and you are particularly fond of young people.

GEMINI WITH VIRGO RISING

You are an excellent communicator with a talent for language, teaching or writing. You can drive yourself crazy worrying about nothing.

GEMINI WITH LIBRA RISING

Convivial and always completely up-to-date in your thinking, you could make a success of a career in the legal profession, or as an international business person.

A Gemini with Taurus rising has a good head for figures and would make a great accountant.

Those Geminis with Pisces rising often work from home.

GEMINI WITH SCORPIO RISING

Far more intense than the average Gemini, you can feel passionate about your beliefs. Your childhood could have left you with a fear of abandonment or financial insecurity.

GEMINI WITH SAGITTARIUS RISING

You seek to protect your personal freedom and you may find it hard to settle down into a conventional lifestyle. You are very excited by ideas and travel.

GEMINI WITH CAPRICORN RISING

You are one of the world's hardest workers, being ambitious for yourself and your family. You may have suffered poverty or deprivation in childhood.

GEMINI WITH AQUARIUS RISING

You are excited by ideas and you may choose a lifestyle which allows you to explore them. You make a career in some form of communications.

GEMINI WITH PISCES RISING

Quieter and more home-loving than the average Gemini, you may be drawn to mystical or psychic matters. You may choose to work from home.

Geminis with Leo rising have an instinctive understanding of children.

The Gemini love of travel is intensified when Sagittarius is rising.

CANCER WITH ARIES RISING

Your tough outer manner hides a soft core. You care for the underdog but you have no patience with people who won't help themselves.

CANCER WITH TAURUS RISING

You could be very keen on art, or music, and may also be a creative cook. You need money in the bank and a loving family around you.

CANCER WITH GEMINI RISING

Your go-getting nature gives you more outer confidence than the average Cancerian. You could study history, or write about it for a living.

CANCER WITH CANCER RISING

This is the purest form of the sign of Cancer, so its characteristics are very strong. You are caring, home-loving and quite money-minded. Your moods fluctuate, especially if you were born after dawn. You will be more fiery, self-centered and outgoing if born before dawn

CANCER WITH LEO RISING

You are more outgoing than the average Cancerian, but you also have a desire to explore your inner life and to find meanings for everything.

CANCER WITH VIRGO RISING

Interested in health and healing, you may be drawn to the medical world, or seek to help those who are weak or needy.

CANCER WITH LIBRA RISING

A Cancerian with Taurus rising is an excellent creative cook.

This is quite a powerful combination, which makes for a successful person with a very charming nature. You would thoroughly enjoy family life, as long as you could have a career too.

CANCER WITH SCORPIO RISING

You are extremely intuitive, sensitive, and easily hurt, although, you can be tough and determined when you need.

CANCER WITH SAGITTARIUS RISING

Your career is important to you, but home is where your heart is. You need a deeply committed personal relationship alongside your freedom.

CANCER WITH CAPRICORN RISING

Your parents are a strong influence, and you may follow them into the family business. You have a strong need for personal and financial security.

CANCER WITH AQUARIUS RISING

Your idealistic streak could lead you to work for needy people, for animals, or as a teacher. You guard your home life and keep it private.

CANCER WITH PISCES RISING

You are extremely sensitive and probably also psychic. Your family means a lot to you. Religion or mysticism may interest you.

A Cancerian with Pisces rising has a strong religious sense.

When Cancer is combined with Gemini rising there is a great love of history.

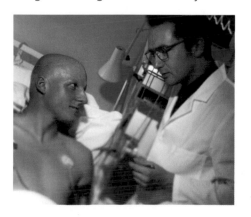

The mixture of Cancer with Virgo rising gives an interest in medical matters.

LEO WITH ARIES RISING

This fiery combination brings a childlike innocence to a courageous personality. You could be a great leader, an idealist, or simply a happy family person with a nice home.

LEO WITH TAURUS RISING

You have a stubborn and determined personality and, when you put your mind to it, you can accomplish a good deal. Family life is very important to you.

LEO WITH GEMINI RISING

This sparkling combination makes for a sharp wit, in combination with a kind heart. You could use your creative imagination to make music, write stories, or entertain children.

LEO WITH CANCER RISING

You love family life and may be very attached to your parents. Your fears, phobias, and feelings are well hidden.

Strong family values are associated with Leo with Aries rising.

LEO WITH LEO RISING

This is Leo in its purest form, so what people see is what they get. You are courageous, but not always as confident as you look, especially if you were born after the Sun had risen. You would be more outgoing if born before dawn.

LEO WITH VIRGO RISING

Your nature has two sides to it, with part of you being lighthearted, and part being deeply serious. You may be keen on new-age matters, or work in the media.

LEO WITH LIBRA RISING

This combination makes for a relaxed and rather lazy personality. You may be happy to let your charm and good looks do your work for you most of the time.

LEO WITH SCORPIO RISING

This intense combination makes for a strong and determined personality who wants to get to the top. You may look like a career person, but you need plenty of love and affection too.

The combination of Leo with Gemini rising is a very creative one.

LEO WITH SAGITTARIUS RISING

You are quick to think and to act. You enjoy travel and you may choose to work in the travel or tourist industry. You need personal freedom alongside love and affection.

LEO WITH CAPRICORN RISING

This powerful combination makes for a very hard worker. Your emotions are deep and you care passionately about your beliefs, and about those whom you love.

LEO WITH AQUARIUS RISING

You may be wrapped up in work or in causes. You have a strong and stubborn personality although this is accompanied by a great sense of humor and plenty of love in your life.

LEO WITH PISCES RISING

This combination could take you into the medical field or into caring professions. You are split between a desire to sacrifice yourself for others and to live for yourself.

A union of mind, body, and spirit are achieved when Leo has Virgo rising.

The mix of Virgo with Capricorn rising gives patience and ability to do detailed work such as accounting.

VIRGO WITH ARIES RISING

You appear more outgoing than most Virgos but you are actually shy and unsure of yourself underneath your outgoing exterior. You could be drawn to teaching or hospital work.

VIRGO WITH TAURUS RISING

Your artistic eye could attract you to work in the fashion business or to restaurant and hotel work. You appreciate anything that feels and looks good.

VIRGO WITH GEMINI RISING

This gives you a very quick mind and a rather sarcastic tongue, but your sense of humor makes up for this. You would make an excellent journalist or broadcaster.

VIRGO WITH CANCER RISING

You have a very soft heart and you may be fond of animals. You could be fascinated by history or genealogy. You may teach and/or work close to home.

Virgos with Sagittarius rising are more interested in sports than are other Virgoans.

Inset: A Virgo with Scorpio rising often possesses an unreadable "poker face".

VIRGO WITH LEO RISING

With a dynamic personality and real executive ability, you have a soft center and you need a gentle partner who makes you feel secure.

VIRGO WITH VIRGO RISING

This is Virgo in its purest form, therefore, you have a talent for detailed work and also for working in any kind of communication field. Your nerves are sensitive, especially if you were born after the sun had risen. You would be tougher and more outgoing if born before dawn.

VIRGO WITH LIBRA RISING

You are a strange mixture of gentle sensitivity and pure dynamism. You care deeply for friends and relatives, and may have a mystical or religious outlook on life.

VIRGO WITH SCORPIO RISING

You could be shy and retiring, and you may cover this up by an inexpressive look on your face. Under this blank-looking exterior, you have deep and rather unhappy feelings.

VIRGO WITH SAGITTARIUS RISING

Your outer manner is friendly and humorous, but you are more ambitious than you look. You could be a keen sports person, animal lover, or a wonderful communicator.

VIRGO WITH CAPRICORN RISING

You are attracted to accountancy, detailed work, or education. You have a serious mind as well as a wonderful sense of humor.

VIRGO WITH AQUARIUS RISING

You may be a rather serious person who never really relaxes. Your mind is active and you have a great deal of curiosity.

VIRGO WITH PISCES RISING

Your early life could have been rather lonely, which makes you turn inward and develop your imagination and psychic powers.

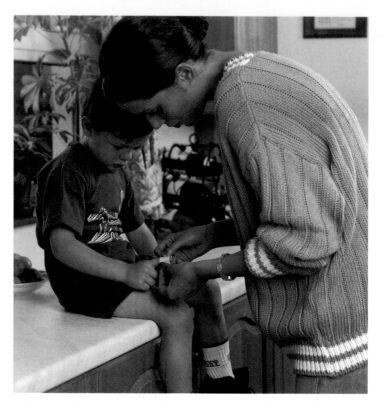

Librans with Cancer rising often make great sacrifices for the sake of their families.

LIBRA WITH ARIES RISING

This combination brings great potential for success, but you may not be able to finish all that you start, due to laziness or impatience with details.

LIBRA WITH TAURUS RISING

This is an artistic combination, which also endows you with the ability to cope with details. You love music, cooking, or gardening.

LIBRA WITH GEMINI RISING

You are an excellent communicator and you may be drawn to legal work or broadcasting. You could be very good looking, too.

LIBRA WITH CANCER RISING

Your family is important to you, and you make considerable sacrifices for them. You may work from home, or in a restaurant, or hotel.

Librans with Aquarius rising are often keen on computing and electronics in general.

LIBRA WITH LEO RISING

You love the worlds of business and glamor, as well as the good things of life. You could be good looking and very musical, and you have a great sense of humor.

LIBRA WITH VIRGO RISING

This combination makes for a very dynamic personality, but you also enjoy family life. You love cooking, gardening, and socializing.

LIBRA WITH LIBRA RISING

This is Libra in its purest form. You should be good looking, rather glamorous, and lazy, until something comes along that holds your interest. Flirtatious and indecisive, you would be kinder if born before dawn than if born after the sun had risen.

LIBRA WITH SCORPIO RISING

Idealistic, you are attracted to politics and may work for the benefit of humanity, sacrificing your own needs in the meantime.

LIBRA WITH SAGITTARIUS RISING

Freedom and fair play is very important to you. You may choose to work in the legal profession, in teaching, or something religious or spiritual.

LIBRA WITH CAPRICORN RISING

This strong combination could make you a very successful business person, but you must try to balance this with a good family life.

LIBRA WITH AQUARIUS RISING

With an active mind you may be extremely intellectual and you can use this to help others. You may be keen on computers and electronics. Guard against letting things slide.

A combination of Libra and Taurus rising gives two doses of the ruling planet Venus so "green fingers" are to be expected.

Librans with Pisces rising are usually dreamy or "otherworldly".

LIBRA WITH PISCES RISING

You could be keen on fashion, photography or anything artistic or beautiful. You are probably good looking with a dreamy, unworldly appearance.

There is a sense of isolation about a Scorpio who has Pisces rising. They nevertheless fear abandonment.

Inset: Scorpio with Gemini rising might be attracted to work in unusual fields such as forensics.

SCORPIO WITH ARIES RISING

This powerful combination belongs to a soldier or a person who fights for truth and justice. You may miss out on family life a bit.

SCORPIO WITH TAURUS RISING

You need to love and be loved, but you may have to wait until the right person comes along. You are stubborn, but probably not difficult to live with.

SCORPIO WITH GEMINI RISING

You are attracted to work in unusual fields, such as forensics or some other kind of investigative job. Your nerves are delicate.

SCORPIO WITH CANCER RISING

Home and family are important, but you are also restless and love to travel over water. You have a great deal of charm and a likeable personality.

SCORPIO WITH LEO RISING

This powerful combination makes you a true leader. You may choose a military life or something similar. You have impossibly high standards.

SCORPIO WITH VIRGO RISING

You are deeply intellectual and you may be keen on medical work, or the creation of music or literature. You must watch your sharp tongue.

SCORPIO WITH LIBRA RISING

This combination attracts you to legal work or, at least to the idea of fair play for all. You could be interested in politics or in helping humanity.

SCORPIO WITH SCORPIO RISING

This is Scorpio in its purest form. Your feelings are intensely passionate and you take life seriously. People either love you or hate you. You would be even more intuitive if born after the sun had risen, and rather more tough and outgoing if born before dawn.

SCORPIO WITH SAGITTARIUS RISING

You are drawn to mystical or psychic matters and may be quite eccentric at times. You will travel and meet many interesting people.

SCORPIO WITH CAPRICORN RISING

You need personal and financial security and you will work hard to get it. You are career minded, but you also have a good social life.

SCORPIO WITH AQUARIUS RISING

Work is important to you. You could be drawn to medical or investigative work. You have plenty of friends and an interesting life. You are stubborn.

SCORPIO WITH PISCES RISING

Your feelings are strong and sensitive. You fear loss or abandonment, although you can enjoy your own company when you choose to.

Sagittarius rising gives a love of travel and the exotic.

Above: A very determined picture emerges when there is a double dose of Scorpio. Life is taken very seriously indeed.

SAGITTARIUS WITH LEO RISING

This fiery combination makes for an outgoing and confident character. You may be a wonderful leader, but you lack confidence in matters of love.

SAGITTARIUS WITH VIRGO RISING

You may have had a difficult childhood but you are happier later on. You would enjoy working in the media or the travel trade.

SAGITTARIUS WITH LIBRA RISING

You are artistic and you may be a great cook. You love meeting new people and you probably have many friends. Psychic matters interest you.

SAGITTARIUS WITH ARIES RISING

This fiery combination makes for an outgoing personality. You may have difficulty in finishing all that you start or in coping with details.

SAGITTARIUS WITH TAURUS RISING

There are many sides to your personality and you may be best able to express it in your job. You love the outdoor life and gardening.

SAGITTARIUS WITH GEMINI RISING

You are a terrific communicator and a wonderful teacher, but you may not stay still long enough to develop deep personal relationships.

SAGITTARIUS WITH CANCER RISING

You are quieter than the average Sagittarian and although you enjoy traveling, you also need a stable home life with a family to stand by you.

A Sagittarian with Taurus rising loves the outdoor life and is often keen on gardening.

SAGITTARIUS WITH SCORPIO RISING

This powerful combination could make you a top politician or sportsman. You will always be larger than life and probably great fun to be with.

SAGITTARIUS WITH SAGITTARIUS RISING

This is Sagittarius in its purest form. You are keen on exploration of either a mental, spiritual, or physical kind. You have a great sense of humor. You would be very psychic if born after the sun had risen and more outgoing if born before dawn.

Unconventional therapies usually fascinate a Sagittarian with Aquarius rising.

SAGITTARIUS WITH CAPRICORN RISING

You are rather quiet and shy for a Sagittarian, and you could be deeply spiritual. You have a head for business and may be keen on math.

SAGITTARIUS WITH AQUARIUS RISING

Ideas fascinate you and you could be a keen astrologer or natural therapist. You are extremely eccentric and you are unlikely to live a dull or boring life.

SAGITTARIUS WITH PISCES RISING

You are gentle, kind, and rather mystical. It takes you a while to find a lifestyle that suits you, and you will probably end up helping others.

Mutable signs often indicate a difficult childhood. This is the case when a Sagittarian has Virgo or Gemini rising

CAPRICORN WITH LEO RISING

Work is important, but you also enjoy family and social life. You are more outgoing than the average Capricorn. You may be keen on alternative health ideas.

CAPRICORN WITH VIRGO RISING

You have a great sense of humor which probably saves you from being too serious. You are capable of doing very detailed work, and anything relating to health and healing appeals to you.

CAPRICORN WITH ARIES RISING

This powerful combination makes for a top politician or a captain of industry, although home and family are also very important to you.

CAPRICORN WITH TAURUS RISING

You are extremely sensual and probably quite artistic. You may be keen on cooking, gardening, music, dancing, or any practical application of creative ideas.

CAPRICORN WITH GEMINI RISING

You may live for work and forget to have a personal life, but you have a great sense of humor and you are a wonderful communicator.

CAPRICORN WITH CANCER RISING

This gentle combination makes you a wonderful family member. You are more ambitious than you look and you also want your family to get on in life.

A Capricorn with Gemini rising has a wonderful sense of humor.

CAPRICORN WITH LIBRA RISING

This combination could make you a business whiz-kid or simply the power behind somebody else's throne. You can use your artistic talent in practical ways.

CAPRICORN WITH SCORPIO RISING

You could be an aggressive money-maker with executive abilities. However, you are equally interested in music, literature, and what makes the world tick.

CAPRICORN WITH SAGITTARIUS RISING

You are more outgoing than the average Capricorn, with a sense of adventure and a fondness for travel and meeting interesting, new people.

CAPRICORN WITH CAPRICORN RISING

This is Capricorn in its purest form, therefore you are hard-working, patient, thorough, and capable of coping with details. You probably had a hard or lonely childhood. You would be more introverted if born after dawn than if you were born before.

CAPRICORN WITH AQUARIUS RISING

This unusual combination makes you sensitive, intuitive, and interested in new age ideas. You had a lonely childhood and may not have fitted in either at school or at home.

CAPRICORN WITH PISCES RISING

You enjoy making friends and may run some kind of social club. You are sensitive, rather psychic, and quite gentle, although your mind is very quick and you have a good sense of humor.

Capricorns with Sagittarius rising have a yearning for adventure.

Capricorns with Pisces rising make friends easily and may run a social club of some kind.

Capricorns with Libra rising can use their creativity in practical ways.

A double dose of Aquarius makes a person very individualistic, sometimes to the point of eccentricity.

AQUARIUS WITH ARIES RISING

You are fairly outgoing and have many friends and acquaintances. You enjoy working in large organizations or in a job where you can advise people.

AQUARIUS WITH TAURUS RISING

This combination makes for a stubborn and determined individual, leading you to choose a way of life and then stick to it. You are attracted to the arts and to literature.

AQUARIUS WITH GEMINI RISING

Bright and breezy, intelligent and aware, you are great company and you have many friends, but you are also quite ambitious. You may travel in order to learn about people.

AQUARIUS WITH CANCER RISING

You may work in teaching, nursing, counseling, or something similar. You are gentler and more family-minded than most Aquarians.

AQUARIUS WITH LEO RISING

You are outgoing and full of fun, you need to enjoy life, and you could also be very ambitious. Computer work may attract you and you would also make a very good astrologer.

AQUARIUS WITH VIRGO RISING

Health and healing appeal to you, so you may take up aromatherapy or something similar. You work hard when you find something that interests you.

AQUARIUS WITH LIBRA RISING

You are intelligent, charming, and good looking, all of which help you achieve your ambitions. Creative and inventive, you are fond of children.

AQUARIUS WITH SCORPIO RISING

You choose a way of life and then stick to it, even when it doesn't really work. You are stubborn, determined, but also helpful to those who are unhappy or in pain.

AQUARIUS WITH SAGITTARIUS RISING

You could be a real oddball, being split between materialistic and spiritual goals. You love learning new things and your interests are wide ranging and unusual.

AQUARIUS WITH CAPRICORN RISING

This combination gives you executive ability and a go-getting nature. Your confidence is not all that it seems and you need a steady partner to give you security.

An Aquarian with Virgo or Scorpio rising desires to help those in pain.

A double dose of Aquarius makes a person very individualistic sometimes to the point of eccentricity.

AQUARIUS WITH AQUARIUS RISING

This is Aquarius in its purest form, therefore you are independent, eccentric and intelligent. You choose unusual jobs and have many interesting friends. You would be quieter, gentler, and quite psychic if born after dawn, but tougher and more outgoing if born before the Sun had risen.

AQUARIUS WITH PISCES RISING

Mysticism and psychic matters appeal to you, partly because you are sensitive, but also because you are attracted to mysticism. You could have been lonely when young.

PISCES WITH ARIES RISING

You are more outgoing than the average Aries, but you can be reclusive at times. You could very sensitive to atmospheres and even clairvoyant at times.

PISCES WITH TAURUS RISING

You could do very well financially during your life. You are very creative and could find work in the arts, especially in the music industry.

PISCES WITH GEMINI RISING

You are brighter and more outgoing than most Pisceans, and you could be very ambitious too. You may have been abandoned or unloved as a child.

Pisces with Taurus rising is usually an indication of prosperity.

Pisceans with Libra rising alternate between being dreamy and practical.

PISCES WITH CANCER RISING

This combination makes for an excellent teacher or counsellor. You are very sensitive and inclined to complain to others about your problems.

PISCES WITH LEO RISING

You are stubborn and determined, but also a real softy with a kind heart. You could be quite clairvoyant and also artistic. You could work in music or the arts.

PISCES WITH VIRGO RISING

Be careful not to lumber yourself with people who need rescuing, because they will drain you. Your early life may have been lonely or unhappy.

PISCES WITH LIBRA RISING

You love beauty and may choose to work in fashion, cosmetics, or something similar. You may be lazy and dreamy at times, and quite capable at others.

PISCES WITH SCORPIO RISING

This combination makes you very psychic and keen on mysticism. You are very sensitive, with deep feelings, but you may be so centered on your own needs that you forget those of others.

PISCES WITH SAGITTARIUS RISING

You are very attracted to the spiritual life and you may travel in search of answers. More outgoing than the average Piscean.

PISCES WITH CAPRICORN RISING

A lonely childhood, followed by a life of surprising achievement, as long as you make the effort. You could have been lonely or deprived in some way as a child.

A double dose of Pisces can make a person quite reclusive.

PISCES WITH AQUARIUS RISING

You are more outgoing than the average Piscean, although still very sensitive. You could be a good astrologer or clairvoyant.

PISCES WITH PISCES RISING

This is Pisces in its purest form, therefore, you are dreamy, escapist, artistic, or very clairvoyant. You could work for the benefit of deprived people. You would be extremely reclusive if born after the Sun had risen, but far more outgoing and extroverted if born before dawn.

The houses of the horoscope

By finding your rising sign you have now given an extra dimension to your personal horoscope by creating a whole new "zodiac." This new division of the circle is called the "house" system. The rising sign itself now becomes the first house and is related to the outward expression of your image. The next sign in sequence becomes the second house relating to your possessions and your attitude to them.

You can now fill in the houses on your blank chart (p.29). Start at the rising sign (1) and continue in a counter-clockwise direction, numbering each of the other eleven star signs in turn. A good tip to ensure that you haven't gone wrong is that house seven will be directly across the zodiac circle from house one.

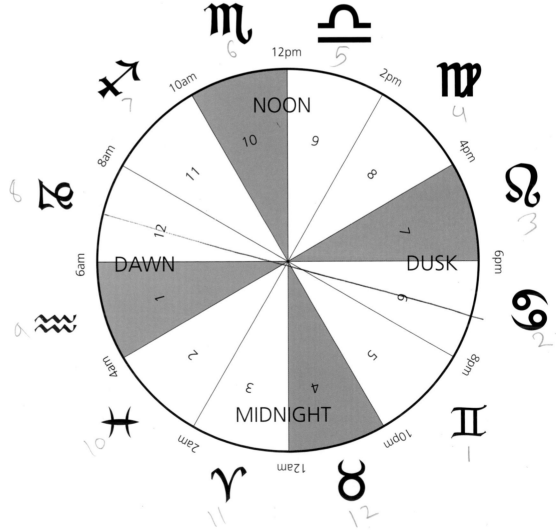

The most important houses are the first, fourth, seventh, and tenth, which represent the way you appear to others (first), where you are from (fourth), what you desire from others (seventh), and where you are going (tenth). To get technical for moment, these houses are called the "angular houses" and any planet found in them will gain extra importance.

The angular houses are very important. The first house (left) or rising sign is associated with image projection, the fourth (top center) with childhood and father figures, the seventh, or setting sign, (bottom center) deals with relationships, while the tenth (right) governs the career.

The sequence of houses is set out below:

First house	Image, outward appearance and how one tends to be perceived by others.
Second house	Possessions, money, and feelings about security issues.
Third house	Communication, early education, local travel and siblings.
Fourth house	Personal background, home life, family, and father figures.
Fifth house	Offspring, creativity, romance, leisure.
Sixth house	Health, habits, and daily work.
Seventh house (setting sign)	Long-term relationships, expectations of partnerships (see the setting sign p.56).
Eighth house	Sexuality, feelings about mortality, inheritance, and shared property or money.
Ninth house	Religious or philosophical opinions, distant travel, higher education.
Tenth house	Ambitions, career, and the main direction in life, also mother figures.
Eleventh house	Friendships, social life, hopes and wishes.
Twelfth house	Seclusion, secrets, and deep psychological issues.

The houses of the horoscope have much in common with the signs of the zodiac from which they are derived. For instance, the influence of the image-conscious first house is very similar to that of the sign of Aries. The materialistic second house is very like Taurus, while the communicative third has an obvious connection to talkative Gemini and so on. This is the reason that in the planetary sections of this book you will find such headings as "Venus in Taurus or the second house" or "Moon in Libra or the seventh house." In short, you can combine the reading for the sign with the reading for the house and thus arrive at a more accurate and extremely personalized astrological portrait.

The first house is like Aries and is image conscious

The second house is like Taurus and is materialistic

The third house is like Gemini and is communicative

The fourth house is like Cancer and is concerned with the past

The fifth house is like Leo and is concerned with creativity

The sixth house is like Virgo and is concerned with health and work

The seventh house is like Libra and is concerned with partnerships

The eighth house is like Scorpio and is concerned with sex

The ninth house is like Sagittarius and is concerned with beliefs

The tenth house is like Capricorn and is concerned with status

The eleventh house is like Aquarius and is concerned with society

The twelfth house is like Pisces and is secretive and mystical

The setting sign

By finding your rising sign you have also found the descendent or "setting sign." This is the star sign directly opposite your rising sign. The descending area of your chart is also very important because, just as the rising sign reveals the way in which you want to be perceived by the world, the setting sign will reveal the qualities that you desire in a potential partner. (The setting sign can also be called the seventh house of partnerships. It has much in common with the sign of Libra.) Many of your closely linked associates, both those of an emotional nature and in professional terms, will exhibit the characteristics of your setting sign. To find out more about your emotional needs in partnership terms turn to the "The Sun sign," pp.17–22 and check out your setting sign.

From top: The 4th house is concerned with memory, heritage and the past in general; the 5th house governs the creative nature, also leisure pursuits, and romantic inclinations; the 9th house is concerned with belief structures, religion, and philosophy; the 11th house is concerned with friendships, ideals, and our place in society.

Finding Your Moon Sign

The Moon is one of the three most important factors in creating an accurate horoscope (the other two being the Sun sign and the rising sign). Seen from the Earth, it is also the fastest moving body in the heavens, and it is therefore impossible to list every possible zodiac position by date alone. To do so would involve a list that would literally fill an entire library.

There is a simple calculation which shows where the Moon was, is, and will be on any date in any year. I know that I promised to do all the hard work for you, and indeed I have, and I promise that this is the most complicated calculation in the whole book. Working out your own Moon sign is not difficult, just follow the procedure step by step.

The following table will give you the zodiac position of the Moon on the first day of your month of birth in your birth year. If you actually happen to have been born on the first of the month you can stop there. However, if you were born on any other day of the month, then another small calculation plus a simple adjustment must be made, by counting along a certain number of star signs according to the date on which you were actually born.

Table 1. The Moon position calculator

Year of birth					Moon's position at the start of your month of birth											
					1	**2**	**3**	**4**	**5**	**6**	**7**	**8**	**9**	**10**	**11**	**12**
1920	1939	1958	1977	1996	TA	CN	CN	VI	LI	SG	CP	AQ	AR	TA	CN	LE
1921	1940	1959	1978	1997	LI	SC	SG	CP	AQ	AR	TA	CN	LE	VI	SC	SG
1922	1941	1960	1979	1998	AQ	AR	AR	GE	CN	LE	VI	SC	CP	AQ	AR	TA
1923	1942	1961	1980	1999	GE	LE	LE	LI	SC	CP	AQ	AR	TA	GE	LE	VI
1924	1943	1962	1981	2000	SC	SG	CP	AQ	AR	TA	GE	LE	LI	SC	SG	CP
1925	1944	1963	1982	2001	PI	TA	TA	CN	LE	LI	SC	SG	AQ	PI	TA	GE
1926	1945	1963	1983	2002	LE	VI	LI	SC	SG	AQ	PI	TA	CN	LE	VI	LI
1927	1946	1964	1984	2003	SG	CP	AQ	PI	TA	GE	LE	VI	SC	SG	AQ	PI
1928	1947	1965	1985	2004	AR	GE	GE	LE	VI	SC	SG	AQ	PI	AR	GE	CN
1929	1948	1966	1986	2005	VI	SC	SC	CP	AQ	PI	TA	GE	LE	VI	LI	SG
1930	1949	1967	1987	2006	CP	PI	PI	TA	GE	LE	VI	SC	SG	CP	PI	AR
1931	1950	1968	1988	2007	TA	CN	CN	VI	LI	SG	CP	PI	AR	GE	CN	LE
1932	1951	1969	1989	2008	LI	SG	SG	AQ	PI	TA	GE	CN	VI	LI	SG	CP
1933	1952	1970	1990	2009	PI	AR	TA	GE	CN	VI	LI	SG	CP	AQ	AR	TA
1934	1953	1971	1991	2010	CN	VI	VI	LI	SG	CP	PI	AR	GE	CN	VI	LI
1935	1954	1972	1992	2011	SC	CP	CP	PI	AR	GE	CN	VI	SC	SG	CP	AQ
1936	1955	1973	1993	2012	AR	TA	GE	LE	VI	LI	SC	CP	PI	AR	TA	CN
1937	1956	1974	1994	2013	LE	LI	LI	SG	CP	PI	AR	TA	CN	LE	LI	SC
1938	1957	1975	1995	2014	CP	AQ	PI	AR	TA	CN	LE	LI	SC	CP	AQ	AR

Key (alphabetical): AQ = Aquarius, AR = Aries, CP = Capricorn, CN = Cancer, GE = Gemini,

LE = Leo, LI = Libra, PI = Pisces, SC = Scorpio, SG = Sagittarius, TA = Taurus, VI = Virgo)

Table 2. Star signs to be added for each day of the month

So, if you were born on August 17, 1984, then the position of the Moon at the beginning of August was Virgo. The 17th corresponds to number 7 in Table 2 (right), so count along seven star signs from Virgo, which brings us to Aries. Therefore the Moon was in the sign of Aries on August 17, 1984.

The Sun was in Virgo (left) and the Moon in Aries (below) on August 17, 1974.

Day of the month	Number of star signs to be added on	List of star signs for your reference
1	0	Aries
2	1	Taurus
3	1	Gemini
4	1	Cancer
5	2	Leo
6	2	Virgo
7	3	Libra
8	3	Scorpio
9	4	Sagittarius
10	4	Capricorn
11	5	Aquarius
12	5	Pisces
13	5	Aries
14	6	Taurus
15	6	Gemini
16	7	Cancer
17	7	Leo
18	8	Virgo
19	8	Libra
20	9	Scorpio
21	9	Sagittarius
22	10	Capricorn
23	10	Aquarius
24	10	Pisces
25	11	
26	11	
27	0	
28	0	
29	1	
30	1	
31	2	

The signs of the zodiac

This simple calculation of the Moon's position works about 80 percent of the time. If, after reading the interpretation of your birth Moon, you think that it doesn't fit your emotional make-up at all, then look at the interpretations for the signs on either side of it. You will probably find that one of those fits you much better. If this is the case then that sign is most likely to be your own Moon sign.

Now it's your turn. First find your year of birth in Table 1 (p.59). Follow the line across until you find your month of birth. This will reveal where the Moon was on the first day of that month. Note this star sign here....

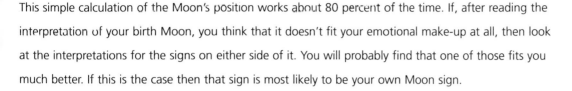

MOON SIGN ON THE FIRST DAY OF THE MONTH:

Now look up your date of birth in Table 2 (previous page). Next to this date there is a number. Note this number here...

(if you were born on the 1st, 26th or 27th you can stop here because no further calculation is necessary).

NUMBER OF STAR SIGNS TO BE ADDED ON:

Now refer to the right-hand column of Table 2 (List of star signs). Begin at the Moon sign on the first day of the month and count down the star signs until you arrive at the number you found in Table 2.

YOUR MOON SIGN IS:

EXAMPLE

To find the Moon sign on January 30, 2002 look up that year in Table 1. Find the relevant month, in this case "1" and read the Moon's position on the first day of that month. It is Leo.

					1	2	3	4	5	6	7	8	9I	10	11	12
1924	1943	1962	1981	2000	SC	SG	CP	AQ	AR	TA	GE	LE	LI	SC	SG	CP
1925	1944	1963	1982	2001	PI	TA	TA	CN	LE	LI	SC	SG	AQ	PI	TA	GE
1926	1945	1963	1983	(2002)	LE	VI	LI	SC	SG	AQ	PI	TA	CN	LE	VI	LI
1927	1946	1964	1984	2003	SG	CP	AQ	PI	TA	GE	LE	VI	SC	SG	AQ	PI
1928	1947	1965	1985	2004	AR	GE	GE	LE	VI	SC	SG	AQ	PI	AR	GE	CN

Now refer to Table 2 to find what adjustment has to be made for the date. The 30th of the month corresponds to the number 1, so one star sign has to be added to Leo to find the Moon sign.

The answer is the very next star sign in the sequence which is Virgo. So on January 30, 2002, the Moon was to be found in the sign of Virgo.

26	11
27	0
28	0
29	1
30	(1)
31	2

					1	2	3	4	5	6	7	8	9I	10	11	12
1924	1943	1962	1981	2000	SC	SG	CP	AQ	AR	TA	GE	LE	LI	SC	SG	CP
1925	1944	1963	1982	2001	PI	TA	TA	CN	LE	LI	SC	SG	AQ	PI	TA	GE
1926	1945	1963	1983	2002	LE	(VI)	LI	SC	SG	AQ	PI	TA	CN	LE	VI	LI
1927	1946	1964	1984	2003	SG	CP	AQ	PI	TA	GE	LE	VI	SC	SG	AQ	PI
1928	1947	1965	1985	2004	AR	GE	GE	LE	VI	SC	SG	AQ	PI	AR	GE	CN

Once you have completed that task you can draw the Moon symbol in the correct sign on your personal horoscope chart.

The Moon in the signs and houses

THE MOON IN ARIES OR THE FIRST HOUSE

This is quite a selfish or rather self-centered placement for the Moon. The "me-first" attitude of Aries is strongly emphasized. Quick to make up their mind, but often changeable in opinions, these individuals may be regarded as wilful or awkward. Very emotional, with deep loves and hates, there is much genuine enthusiasm, but patience is lacking and must be consciously developed. There may also be a difficulty in accepting discipline and with dealing with authority figures. The one exception to this is in the case of the mother to whom the subject will be very close.

The only authority figure that a Lunar Aries tolerates is his mother.

THE MOON IN TAURUS OR THE SECOND HOUSE

The Moon is regarded as being "exalted" when in Taurus, and, indeed, the inconstancy of the lunar force is stabilized when it is found here. The Moon in this sign or house is favorable for financial interests, even though there will be periods when there are fluctuations in the income. On the whole, this lunar position is a positive one, granting optimism, practicality, and a hopeful outlook. There will be a love of luxury and the subject will be physically sensual. A lunar Taurean is likely to be possessive of individuals and property alike.

The Moon in Taurus is favorable to financial interests.

THE MOON IN GEMINI OR THE THIRD HOUSE

The Moon is never more changeable than when it is found in the fickle sign of Gemini. This is an indication of considerable restlessness and possibly of indecisiveness, although there is a genuine ability to take on many tasks at once, to allocate time to each, to handle each efficiently, and get them all finished on schedule. Nothing could be more boring than concentrating on one thing at a time! This person may have had an unsettled education and will be very protective of siblings and friends. Nervous tension may cause a problem for someone with the Moon in this position.

Lunar Geminians are easily bored and like to handle many tasks at once.

THE MOON IN CANCER OR THE FOURTH HOUSE

The Moon is the ruling planet of Cancer and is therefore described as "dignified" when it occupies this, its natural home. The most obvious feature is a strong maternal (or paternal) sense, with powerful instincts, and an intuitive understanding of someone else's needs. This is a good indicator for the subject's domestic life as well as for family relationships. However, the apron strings may be uncomfortably tight, and this individual is likely to be possessive and clingy to loved ones. There may also be an interest in history, family background, or collecting antiques.

The Moon is very strong in its own sign of Cancer, so is likely to promote possessiveness of loved ones.

THE MOON IN LEO OR THE FIFTH HOUSE

Here the Moon grants a 'sunny' disposition, popularity and self-confidence. Others will look to this person for leadership and decision-making abilities, although there may be a tendency to try to run other people's lives for them. There is a strong inclination to artistic talent in this person and this will usually manifest itself as a quite unique ability. People with the Moon in this sign or house may achieve fame through their gifts and undoubted popularity with the public as a whole. Loyalty is a strong feature, as is a self-indulgent love of the good life.

Lunar Leos are popular, artistically gifted and may achieve great fame.

THE MOON IN VIRGO OR THE SIXTH HOUSE

There is usually a deep-seated insecurity in someone with the Moon in Virgo probably resulting from unsettled conditions in childhood. The sense of duty to others will be very strong and extremely demanding because this person feels the need to justify his existence by serving those around him. This individual may be nervy, rather timid and prone to stomach upsets when under stress. In business terms the lunar Virgoan will score highly because their meticulousness and dutiful attitudes will ensure long-term success.

The Moon in Virgo can promote insecurity and needless worry.

THE MOON IN LIBRA OR THE SEVENTH HOUSE

The highly romantic placement of the Moon in Libra or the seventh house can cause emotional problems, simply because their expectations of a prospective partner may be far too high. Lunar Librans sometimes fall in love with love rather than with any particular individual, and may want to be mothered in a relationship. This person is a shrewd judge of character, however, and gets on better with women than he or she does with men.

Lunar Librans keep falling in love with love rather than any single person.

THE MOON IN SCORPIO OR THE EIGHTH HOUSE

The Moon is not at all happy in Scorpio where is it described as being in "fall." The emotions, therefore, are likely to be very intense, and this lunar subject can be extremely demanding. Personal standards of behavior will be high, and so will their expectations of others. If, as often happens, other people cannot live up to this, then moodiness and resentment can result. This person may appear to be introverted, but still waters run deep and the quiet exterior masks an inner turbulence

The lunar Scorpio emotions tend to be intense and turbulent.

THE MOON IN SAGITTARIUS OR THE NINTH HOUSE

The inconstant Moon is even more restless than usual when found in the mutable sign of Sagittarius. This is an optimistic, cheerful sort of person, with a broad mind, independent attitudes, and a strong desire for freedom. Philosophical in attitude, this subject is sometimes so preoccupied with abstract thought that he can seem to be aloof or off-hand. However, he has a good heart and a very good brain, with an ability to study deeply. Many changes of residence are often a feature in the life of this individual. He or she may have a foreign parental background and is often psychic.

Lunar Sagittarians are restless and freedom-loving.

THE MOON IN CAPRICORN OR THE TENTH HOUSE

The cold, ambitious Capricorn is not a comfortable position for the Moon which is described as being in "detriment" when it is found here. The Moon stabilizes the emotions when in this sign, so lunar Capricorns are diligent, prudent, and careful. It is to be hoped that these excellent qualities are not taken so far that prudence becomes pessimism and caution austerity. It must be said that there is a lot of common sense and responsibility in this type, even if he or she does need cheering up now and again.

Pessimistic lunar Capricorns often need distraction to cheer them up.

THE MOON IN AQUARIUS OR THE ELEVENTH HOUSE

This must be the most unpredictable and eccentric placement for the Moon in the entire zodiac. Lunar Aquarians could be almost anything! They break the rules and are exactly what they want to be when they want to be it! Original, ingenious and independent, they often prefer to live alone simply because others make too many demands on them. They can appear to be both bohemian and snobbish at the same time, and there may be a total incomprehension of what image they actually convey to others. Nevertheless, this is a fascinating person.

Lunar Aquarians often prefer an unconventional, bohemian lifestyle.

THE MOON IN PISCES OR THE TWELFTH HOUSE

The first word that springs to mind when describing a lunar Piscean is psychic! This is the most sensitive placement for the Moon and the individual who possesses it is so receptive to outside influences that the unconscious mind is flooded with information from both material and more subtle sources. Very imaginative, this person is gentle, kindly and very friendly. This is one who needs to be liked and hates confrontations and pushy people. Often too easily discouraged, this subject needs reassurance and a loving atmosphere to flourish.

Moon in Pisces people are usually quite psychic and receptive.

THE PLANETS

The inner planets are the ones in the Earth's immediate 'family': Mercury, Venus, Mars, Jupiter and Saturn. These are the planets that have a marked effect on our day-to-day lives. The Sun, Moon and rising sign provide the background to the birth chart, and the positions of the inner planets fill in further details.

The inner planets

Mercury is specifically concerned with the intellect and with the ability to communicate one's thoughts. This planet moves so quickly in its orbit that it is impossible to list its positions, but since it is so close to the Sun, you can assume that it is in the same sign as the Sun or in the sign on either side of it.

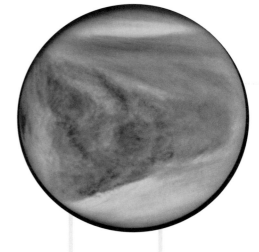

Venus is not only the planet of love, but is also concerned with money and the way in which we regard our possessions. The positions of Venus are listed on pp.84–89.

Mars is best known as the planet of war, but also governs personal drive, energy levels, and effort. The positions of Mars are listed on pp.95–98.

Jupiter is known as the "luck-bringer" and is concerned with good fortune, but also with optimism, travel, study, religion, and philosophy. Jupiter's positions are listed on pp.106–107.

Saturn is often regarded as the gloomy author of all our ills, yet without it we would have no self-discipline and learn none of life's lessons. Saturn's positions are listed on p.113.

The inner planets are very important and you should take the trouble to look up their positions at the time of your birth and mark them in on your horoscope sheet. For further information about the generation you were born into and the influence that era has had on your life, look at the distant and slow-moving outer planets.

The distant planets

Uranus, Neptune, and Pluto move so slowly that they influence whole generations of humanity. It takes Uranus 84 years to orbit the Sun, Neptune 168 years 292 days, and Pluto 248 years 183 days. Therefore, it is not really necessary to interpret their influence in a sign of the zodiac, when considering a single individual. However, they do also have a house position that is unique to each person, and relationships to the other planets, so they cannot be ignored. The positions of Uranus, Neptune and Pluto are listed on p.123.

Mercury in the signs and houses

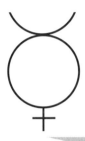

Throughout this book you will find lists of planetary positions or simple formulae to find the positions of planets within your personal birth chart. The swift-moving planet Mercury, which governs the intellect and the capacity for communication, is an exception, however. It is impossible to list every time that this planet changes sign because it does so far too often to be included in a book of this size. On the other hand, Mercury is the planet which orbits closest to the Sun so therefore it cannot be too far away from our parent star. In short, in most cases Mercury will occupy the same sign as the Sun, but you may want to read the entries for the signs on either side of your Sun sign to see if the characteristics of these fit your intellectual nature better.

If your Sun is in Gemini or Virgo then Mercury is your ruling planet and is therefore far more important than to individuals with other Sun signs. If you want to know more about Mercury and its influence invest in an astrological computer program or consult a reputable astrologer.

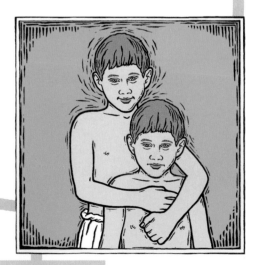 

The perceptive, intellectual nature of Mercury is reflected in the two signs which it rules, Gemini and Virgo.

Mercury in Aries or the first house

These subjects may be very clever and literate or conversely they may find thinking, talking or writing difficult. The same applies to numeracy: they could be computer and accounts experts or, equally, unable to cope with numbers. They try to make an intellectual impact on the world. Some overrule feelings with logic. Their thinking may be too diverse or too self-centred.

Mercury in Taurus or the second house

Businesslike and business-minded, these people make great traders and dealers. Practical and dextrous, they can be good craftsmen or musicians, and are interested in food and cookery. They are keen on education and make good teachers.

Mercury in Gemini or the third house

(Mercury is described as being 'dignified' and therefore very strong when in Gemini.)
They may be closely involved with brothers and sisters, neighbours or neighbourhood matters. Local travel and vehicles could figure strongly in their lives. They may release pent-up tension by writing poetry or music.

When Mercury is in Aries the subject is often very good with figures and quick on the uptake.

Mercury in its own sign of Gemini implies closeness to brothers and sisters.

Mercury in Taurus often indicates an interest in food and gourmet cookery.

Mercury in Cancer or the fourth house

These subjects are fond of their home surroundings and they may choose to work from home. Maternal and domesticated, they make a point of talking and listening to their children, and they are also keen on educating them. These people may be interested in history, or in collecting things which have a past. They can work from home as counselors or "agony aunts" (or astrologers). They may teach or become involved with children.

Those with Mercury in Cancer make a point of communicating with their children.

Mercury in Leo or the fifth house

Good at intellectual games, they may be easily bored by work that requires attention to detail or a rigid routine. They want both love and sex, and they see sex as an essential part of communication. They also need a lover with whom they can really talk.

Mercury in Virgo or the sixth house

(Mercury is both "dignified" and "exalted" in Virgo, and therefore extremely powerful.) These subjects have very analytical minds and they make excellent secretaries. They can be academic, musical, or good at craft and design. They may be nervous, fussy or health-conscious. They find it hard to plan or to look forward with optimism, and they may suffer from low self-esteem. Some talk incessantly about nothing.

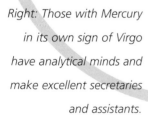

Right: Those with Mercury in its own sign of Virgo have analytical minds and make excellent secretaries and assistants.

Far right: People with Mercury in Leo usually loathe a rigid routine.

Mercury in Libra or the seventh house

These subjects seek an intellectual rapport with others. They are good friends and also excellent diplomats or liaison officers. They have a good attitude to marriage and working partnerships. They may be better talkers than listeners. Some are excellent designers or craftsmen. If Mercury is afflicted, these subjects may be prone to illness.

Mercury in Scorpio or the eighth house

They are deep thinkers, and often astute business people. They may be interested in the occult, religion, and the afterlife. They may be keen on reading or writing thrillers, or work in the undertaking industry. Their emotions are deep, but they may be expressed in an intellectual manner. They have good concentration, but an afflicted (with Saturn or Pluto) Mercury can cause blockages in the thinking processes.

Mercury in Sagittarius or the ninth house

(Mercury is in "detriment" here, so quite weak and lacking in focus.)
Good students and teachers with a flair for English or foreign languages. They may have too many ideas to bring any of them to fruition and must learn to apply themselves conscientiously.

Mercury in Scorpio people seeks religious or occult illumination.

Mercury in Capricorn or the tenth house

These individuals can be drawn to a career in communications or a business which has a communicative basis. They need a mental outlet or they may become unhappy or frustrated.

Mercury in Aquarius or the eleventh house

These subjects enjoy being involved with clubs and societies and they have many friends. They are approachable and friendly, although they can be sarcastic and tactless at times. They have wide-ranging ideas about politics.

Mercury in Pisces or the twelfth house

(Mercury is in 'fall' in Pisces and at its least communicative.)
Inward-looking and secretive, their feelings are very important to them. They are sensitive, thoughtful and kind. Some are attracted to mysticism and they may write or compose music on these themes. These people may have problems in connection with their work or their health and they need a happy and stable marriage in order to function successfully.

Mercury in Pisces people may be overly concerned with the state of their health.

Those with Mercury in Capricorn may find a career in the communications industries.

Venus in the signs and houses

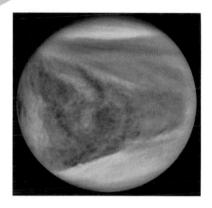

Venus, like the Moon, provides a feminine energy to the birthchart. This planet is associated with the things that we hold dear to us and that we appreciate. Thus Venus is thought of as not only the arbitrator of emotional love but also of money and possessions.

Venus in Aries or the first house

Even though Venus is thought of as being in "detriment" here, this position is an indicator of immense personal charm and beauty, and is considered an excellent planetary placement for models, starlets, and those who work in the glamor or fashion industries. There is usually an interest in art, music, and things of beauty. People with Venus in Aries definitely enjoy flattery and being treated indulgently. There will be a love of luxury and the capacity for being totally pleasure-loving. It is also true that an individual with this Venus position may be lazy.

Those with Venus in the first house are languid, love pleasure, and can have a tendency to be vain.

People with Venus in her own sign of Taurus are adept at making money.

Venus in Taurus or the second house

Venus is powerful when in Taurus because she is the ruler of the sign. Here, Venus exerts a more practical influence, because as well as being interesting in the arts, luxury, and the finer things in life, she also inclines to money-making. Someone with Venus here is usually a good business person with an eye for a bargain and an investment, or possibly a dealer, or a worker in a creative field. They are physically sensual and may be passionate lovers.

Venus in Gemini or the third house

There is a charm and ease to communication when Venus is found in Gemini or the third house. People with Venus in this position have no difficulty in making friends, often wealthy and influential acquaintances. Usually there will be a good relationship with siblings and neighbors. Often extravagant with gifts, this type is not mean and may have a passion for learning. Someone with Venus in Gemini makes a good go-between, liaison officer, or agent of any kind.

Venus in Gemini or the third house maybe extravagent with gifts.

Venus in Cancer or the fourth house need their homes to be tastefully decorated.

Venus in Cancer or the fourth house

A tastefully decorated home is a must for someone with Venus in Cancer or the fourth house. Beauty must surround them, and their environment must be esthetic. Family, too, must come up to scratch and will be rewarded by expressions of affection and generous gifts. Often very emotional, they can be shrewd, especially by investing in collections that will grow in value. They may be very successful in the fields of insurance, property, and the retail trade, and may possess a wealthy or shrewd mother.

Venus in Leo or the fifth house

Those with Venus in Leo or the fifth house will be enormously proud of their children (who are likely to turn out to be rich, successful and glamorous). On a more personal note, this type loves fun and flirtation, love affairs, travel, games, sports, gambling and show-biz. Their gifts extend to being artistically creative, possibly musically talented and never, ever being boring.

Those with Venus in Leo or the fifth house love to have fun wherever they are.

Those with Venus in Virgo will achieve much through hard work and diligence.

Venus in Virgo or the sixth house

As might be imagined, Venus the planet of love is not at home in either the sign of the virgin or the house of duty so is described as being in 'fall'. This type hates dirty work, drudgery and hard physical effort, so will go a long way to avoid these. Desperately needing congenial surroundings, once they are settled in a career they are capable of great efforts. Health conscious, but basically strong, this subject will soldier on and on. The good news is that someone with Venus here will gain considerable influence, material well-being and prestige through work.

Venus in Libra or the seventh house

Venus is very strong in Libra, being the sign's ruler, and is thus described as "dignified." However both Venus's materialistic and amorous natures can be seen here. It's a case of love or money, and usually both at the same time. It could mean that a happy marriage is forecast, or that the partner will be materially successful (not always quite the same thing). It is certain that a person with Venus here will need encouragement to feel validated and reassured. This type is affectionate, warm, and usually extremely romantic.

A happy relationship is usually indicated by a placement of Venus in Libra or the 7th house.

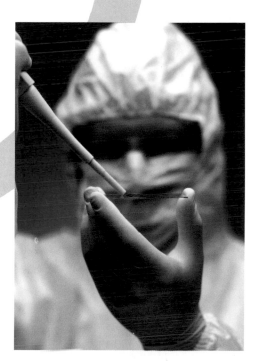

Venus in Scorpio or the eighth house

The amorous passions of Venus take a more negative turn in Scorpio or the eighth house, making this type of person quite jealous and possessive. It can provoke contrasting reactions, either someone completely focused on sex or an individual with no interest in the physical at all. Material wealth often comes through inheritance or marriage. In career terms, anything investigative such as police or medical work would appeal.

Venus in Scorpio or the eighth house gives an interest in investigative work such as police or medical research

Venus in Sagittarius or the ninth house

Travel and learning are the main focuses of a someone with Venus in Sagittarius. Usually open-minded and intelligent, this type does well in higher education. Their travels will take them far and wide, introducing them to other cultures and ways of thinking that they will happily absorb. Often very spiritual in inclination, they may also marry a foreigner or someone from a completely different background to their own. In addition, a second marriage may be more fruitful than the first, and they may be interested in the law, philosophy, or religion.

Venus in Sagittarius or the 9th house gives an open mind and a fascination with other cultures.

Venus in Capricorn or the 10th house gives career status and influential friends.

Venus in Capricorn or the tenth house

Fame and happiness go hand-in-hand with this type. Career status is very important, and this they will win with charm and grace. This type has a very good manner with people and can appeal to a great number. There is a shrewd mind behind all this glamor though, and this subject will always know the right people and have influential friends.

Those with Venus in Aquarius or the 11th house love their social life.

Venus in Aquarius or the eleventh house

Charm and diplomacy are the hallmarks of this type of Venusian personality. The ability to communicate with everyone on their own level, combined with an innate sense of discretion, ensures their almost universal popularity. Usually hating to be alone, this type will find happiness in clubs, societies, and surrounded by like-minded people. Politics may attract this type as much as they are attractive to the well-heeled and influential. Having said that, they are strangers to snobbery and are sincere in their beliefs and causes.

The private life is all-important to those with Venus in Pisces or the 12th house.

Venus in Pisces or the twelfth house

Venus is considered to be "exalted" in Pisces and is instinctive and somewhat primal. Clandestine romance is the secret at the heart of this type of Venusian personality. The last thing that this person wants is to be exposed to public scrutiny. However, this could just be a symptom of a need for seclusion and retreat. There may be an interest in the occult and in mysticism, which could find expression in creative gifts. This is a person who is artistic, musical, and poetic.

Venus calendar 1950–2010

1950
Jan 1	Aquarius
Apr 6	Pisces
May 5	Aries
Jun 1	Taurus
Jun 27	Gemini
Jul 22	Cancer
Aug 16	Leo
Sep 10	Virgo
Oct 4	Libra
Oct 28	Scorpio
Nov 21	Sagittarius
Dec 14	Capricorn

1951
Jan 7	Aquarius
Jan 31	Pisces
Feb 24	Aries
Mar 21	Taurus
Apr 15	Gemini
May 11	Cancer
Jun 8	Leo
Jul 9	Virgo
Nov 9	Libra
Dec 8	Scorpio

1952
Jan 2	Sagittarius
Jan 27	Capricorn
Feb 21	Aquarius
Mar 16	Pisces
Apr 9	Aries
May 4	Taurus
May 28	Gemini
Jun 22	Cancer
Jul 16	Leo
Aug 9	Virgo
Sep 3	Libra
Sep 27	Scorpio
Oct 22	Sagittarius
Nov 15	Capricorn
Dec 10	Aquarius

1953
Jan 5	Pisces
Feb 2	Aries
Mar 14	Taurus
Mar 31	Aries
Jun 5	Taurus
Jul 7	Gemini
Aug 4	Cancer
Aug 30	Leo
Sep 24	Virgo
Oct 18	Libra
Nov 11	Scorpio
Dec 5	Sagittarius
Dec 29	Capricorn

1954
Jan 22	Aquarius
Feb 15	Pisces
Mar 11	Aries
Apr 4	Taurus
Apr 28	Gemini
May 23	Leo
Jul 13	Virgo
Aug 9	Libra
Sep 6	Scorpio
Oct 23	Sagittarius
Oct 27	Scorpio

1955
Jan 6	Sagittarius
Feb 6	Capricorn
Mar 4	Aquarius
Mar 30	Pisces
Apr 24	Aries
May 19	Taurus
Jun 13	Gemini
Jul 8	Cancer
Aug 1	Leo
Aug 25	Virgo
Sep 18	Libra
Oct 13	Scorpio
Nov 6	Sagittarius
Nov 30	Capricorn
Dec 24	Aquarius

1956
Jan 17	Pisces
Feb 11	Aries
Mar 7	Taurus
Apr 4	Gemini
May 8	Cancer
Jun 23	Gemini
Aug 4	Cancer
Sep 8	Leo
Oct 6	Virgo
Oct 31	Libra
Nov 25	Scorpio
Dec19	Sagittarius

1957
Jan 12	Capricorn
Feb 5	Aquarius
Mar 1	Pisces
Mar 25	Aries
Apr 19	Taurus
May 13	Gemini
Jun 6	Cancer
Jul 1	Leo
Jul 26	Virgo
Aug 20	Libra
Sep 14	Scorpio
Oct 10	Sagittarius
Nov 5	Capricorn
Dec 6	Aquarius

1958
Apr 6	Pisces
May 5	Aries
Jun 1	Taurus
Jun 26	Gemini
Jul 22	Cancer
Aug 16	Leo
Sep 9	Virgo
Oct 3	Libra
Oct 27	Scorpio
Nov 20	Sagittarius
Dec 14	Capricorn

1959
Jan 7 — Aquarius
Jan 31 — Pisces
Feb 24 — Aries
Mar 20 — Taurus
Apr 14 — Gemini
May 10 — Cancer
Jun 6 — Leo
Jul 8 — Virgo
Sep 20 — Leo
Sep 25 — Virgo
Nov 9 — Libra
Dec 7 — Scorpio

1960
Jan 2 — Sagittarius
Jan 27 — Capricorn
Feb 20 — Aquarius
Mar 16 — Pisces
Apr 9 — Aries
May 3 — Taurus
May 28 — Gemini
Jun 21 — Cancer
Jul 16 — Leo
Aug 9 — Virgo
Sep 2 — Libra
Sep 27 — Scorpio
Oct 21 — Sagittarius
Nov 15 — Capricorn
Dec 10 — Aquarius

1961
Jan 5 — Pisces
Feb 2 — Aries
Jun 5 — Taurus
Jul 7 — Gemini
Aug 3 — Cancer
Aug 29 — Leo
Sep 23 — Virgo
Oct 18 — Libra
Nov 11 — Scorpio
Dec 5 — Sagittarius
Dec 29 — Capricorn

1962
Jan 21 — Aquarius
Feb 14 — Pisces
Mar 10 — Aries
Apr 3 — Taurus
Apr 28 — Gemini
May 23 — Cancer
Jun 17 — Leo

Jul 12 — Virgo
Aug 8 — Libra
Sep 7 — Scorpio

1963
Jan 6 — Sagittarius
Feb 5 — Capricorn
Mar 4 — Aquarius
Mar 30 — Pisces
Apr 24 — Aries
May 19 — Taurus
Jun 12 — Gemini
Jul 7 — Cancer
Jul 31 — Leo
Aug 25 — Virgo
Sep 18 — Libra
Oct 12 — Scorpio
Nov 5 — Sagittarius
Nov 29 — Capricorn
Dec 23 — Aquarius

1964
Jan 17 — Pisces
Feb 10 — Aries
Mar 7 — Taurus
Apr 4 — Gemini
May 9 — Cancer
Jun 17 — Gemini
Aug 5 — Cancer
Sep 8 — Leo
Oct 5 — Virgo
Oct 31 — Libra
Nov 25 — Scorpio
Dec 19 — Sagittarius

1965
Jan 12 — Capricorn
Feb 5 — Aquarius
Mar 1 — Pisces
Mar 25 — Aries
Apr 18 — Taurus
May 12 — Gemini
Jun 6 — Cancer
Jun 30 — Leo
Jul 15 — Virgo
Aug 19 — Libra
Sep 13 — Scorpio
Oct 9 — Sagittarius
Nov 5 — Capricorn
Dec 7 — Aquarius

1966
Feb 6 — Capricorn
Feb 25 — Aquarius
Apr 6 — Pisces
May 5 — Aries
Jun 26 — Taurus
Jul 21 — Cancer
Aug 15 — Leo
Sep 8 — Virgo
Oct 3 — Libra
Oct 27 — Scorpio
Nov 20 — Sagittarius
Dec 13 — Capricorn

1967
Jan 6 — Aquarius
Jan 30 — Pisces
Feb 23 — Aries
Mar 20 — Taurus
Apr 14 — Gemini
May 10 — Cancer
Jun 8 — Leo
Jul 8 — Virgo
Sep 9 — Leo
Oct 1 — Virgo
Nov 9 — Libra
Dec 7 — Scorpio

1968
Jan 1 — Sagittarius
Jan 26 — Capricorn
Feb 20 — Aquarius
Mar 15 — Pisces
Apr 8 — Aries
May 3 — Taurus
May 27 — Gemini
Jun 21 — Cancer
Jul 15 — Leo
Aug 8 — Virgo
Sep 2 — Libra
Sep 26 — Scorpio
Oct 21 — Sagittarius
Nov 14 — Capricorn
Dec 9 — Aquarius

1969
Jan 4 — Pisces
Feb 2 — Aries
Jun 6 — Taurus
Jul 6 — Gemini
Aug 3 — Cancer
Aug 29 — Leo
Sep 23 — Virgo

1969 (continued)

Oct 17	Libra
Nov 10	Scorpio
Dec 14	Sagittarius
Dec 28	Capricorn

1970

Jan 21	Aquarius
Feb 14	Pisces
Mar 10	Aries
Apr 3	Taurus
Apr 27	Gemini
May 22	Cancer
Jun 16	Leo
Jul 12	Virgo
Aug 8	Libra
Sep 7	Scorpio

1971

Jan 7	Sagittarius
Feb 5	Capricorn
Mar 4	Aquarius
Mar 29	Pisces
Apr 23	Aries
May 18	Taurus
Jun 12	Gemini
Jul 6	Cancer
Jul 31	Leo
Aug 24	Virgo
Sep 17	Libra
Oct 11	Scorpio
Nov 5	Sagittarius
Nov 29	Capricorn
Dec 23	Aquarius

1972

Jan 16	Pisces
Feb 10	Aries
Mar 7	Taurus
May 10	Gemini
Jun 11	Gemini
Aug 6	Cancer
Sep 7	Leo
Oct 5	Virgo
Oct 30	Libra
Nov 24	Scorpio
Dec 18	Sagittarius

1973

Jan 11	Capricorn
Feb 4	Aquarius
Feb 28	Pisces
Mar 24	Aries
Apr 18	Taurus
May 12	Gemini
Jun 5	Cancer
Jun 30	Leo
Jul 25	Virgo
Aug 19	Libra
Sep 13	Scorpio
Oct 9	Sagittarius
Nov 5	Capricorn
Dec 7	Aquarius

1974

Jan 29	Capricorn
Feb 28	Aquarius
Apr 6	Pisces
May 4	Aries
May 31	Taurus
Jun 25	Gemini
Jul 21	Cancer
Aug 14	Leo
Sep 8	Virgo
Oct 2	Libra
Oct 26	Scorpio
Nov 19	Sagittarius
Dec 13	Capricorn

1975

Jan 6	Aquarius
Jan 30	Pisces
Feb 23	Aries
Mar 19	Taurus
Apr 13	Gemini
May 9	Cancer
Jun 6	Leo
Jul 9	Virgo
Sep 2	Leo
Oct 4	Virgo
Nov 9	Libra
Dec 7	Scorpio

1976

Jan 1	Sagittarius
Jan 26	Capricorn
Feb 19	Aquarius
Mar 15	Pisces
Apr 8	Aries
May 2	Taurus
May 27	Gemini

1976 (continued)

Jun 20	Cancer
Jul 14	Leo
Aug 8	Virgo
Sep 1	Libra
Sep 26	Scorpio
Oct 20	Sagittarius
Nov 14	Capricorn
Dec 9	Aquarius

1977

Jan 4	Pisces
Feb 2	Aries
Jun 6	Taurus
Jul 6	Gemini
Aug 2	Cancer
Aug 28	Leo
Sep 22	Virgo
Oct 17	Libra
Nov 10	Scorpio
Dec 4	Sagittarius
Dec 27	Capricorn

1978

Jan 20	Aquarius
Feb 13	Pisces
Mar 9	Aries
Apr	2 Taurus
Apr 27	Gemini
May 22	Cancer
Jun 16	Leo
Jul 12	Virgo
Aug 8	Libra
Sep 7	Scorpio

1979

Jan 7	Sagittarius
Feb 5	Capricorn
Mar 3	Aquarius
Mar 29	Pisces
Apr 23	Aries
May 18	Taurus
Jun 11	Gemini
Jul 6	Cancer
Jul 30	Leo
Aug 24	Virgo
Sep 17	Libra
Oct 11	Scorpio
Nov 4	Sagittarius
Nov 28	Capricorn
Dec 22	Aquarius

1980

Jan 16	Pisces
Feb 9	Aries
Mar 6	Taurus
Apr 3	Gemini
May 12	Cancer
Jun 5	Gemini
Aug 6	Cancer
Sep 7	Leo
Oct 4	Virgo
Oct 30	Libra
Nov 24	Scorpio
Dec 18	Sagittarius

1981

Jan 11	Capricorn
Feb 4	Aquarius
Feb 28	Pisces
Mar 24	Aries
Apr 17	Taurus
May 11	Gemini
Jun 5	Cancer
Jun 29	Leo
Jul 24	Virgo
Aug 18	Libra
Sep 12	Scorpio
Oct 9	Sagittarius
Nov 5	Capricorn
Dec 8	Aquarius

1982

Jan 23	Capricorn
Mar 2	Aquarius
Apr 6	Pisces
May 4	Aries
May 30	Taurus
Jun 25	Gemini
Jul 20	Cancer
Aug 14	Leo
Sep 7	Virgo
Oct 2	Libra
Oct 26	Scorpio
Nov 18	Sagittarius
Dec 12	Capricorn

1983

Jan 5	Aquarius
Jan 29	Pisces
Feb 22	Aries
Mar 19	Taurus
Apr 13	Gemini
May 9	Cancer
Jun 6	Leo

1983 (continued)

Jul 10	Virgo
Aug 27	Leo
Oct 5	Virgo
Nov 9	Libra
Dec 6	Scorpio

1984

Jan 1	Sagittarius
Jan 25	Capricorn
Feb 19	Aquarius
Mar 14	Pisces
Apr 7	Aries
May 2	Taurus
May 26	Gemini
Jun 20	Cancer
Jul 14	Leo
Aug 7	Virgo
Sep 1	Libra
Sep 25	Scorpio
Oct 20	Sagittarius
Nov 13	Capricorn
Dec 9	Aquarius

1985

Jan 2	Pisces
Feb 2	Aries
Jun 6	Taurus
Jul 6	Cancer
Aug 28	Leo
Sep 22	Virgo
Oct 16	Libra
Nov 9	Scorpio
Dec 3	Sagittarius
Dec 27	Capricorn

1986

Jan 20	Aquarius
Feb 13	Pisces
Mar 9	Aries
Apr 2	Taurus
Apr 26	Gemini
May 21	Cancer
Jun 15	Leo
Jul 11	Virgo
Aug 7	Libra
Sep 7	Scorpio

1987

Jan 7	Sagittarius
Feb 5	Capricorn
Mar 3	Aquarius
Mar 28	Pisces

1987 (continued)

Apr 22	Aries
May 17	Taurus
Jun 11	Gemini
Jul 5	Cancer
Jul 30	Leo
Aug 23	Virgo
Sep 16	Libra
Oct 10	Scorpio
Nov 3	Sagittarius
Nov 28	Capricorn
Dec 22	Aquarius

1988

Jan 15	Pisces
Feb 9	Aries
Mar 6	Taurus
Apr 3	Gemini
May 17	Cancer
May 27	Leo
Aug 6	Cancer
Sep 7	Leo
Oct 4	Virgo
Oct 29	Libra
Nov 23	Scorpio
Dec 17	Sagittarius

1989

Jan 10	Capricorn
Feb 3	Aquarius
Feb 27	Pisces
Mar 23	Aries
Apr 16	Taurus
May 11	Gemini
Jun 4	Cancer
Jun 29	Leo
Jul 24	Virgo
Aug 18	Libra
Sep 12	Scorpio
Oct 8	Sagittarius
Nov 5	Capricorn
Dec 10	Aquarius

1990

Jan 16	Capricorn
Mar 3	Aquarius
Apr 6	Pisces
May 4	Aries
May 30	Taurus
Jun 25	Gemini
Jul 20	Cancer
Aug 13	Leo
Sep 7	Virgo

1990 (continued)

Oct 1	Libra
Oct 25	Scorpio
Nov 18	Sagittarius
Dec 12	Capricorn

1991

Jan 5	Aquarius
Jan 29	Pisces
Feb 22	Aries
Mar 18	Taurus
Apr 13	Gemini
May 9	Cancer
Jun 6	Leo
Jul 11	Virgo
Aug 21	Leo
Oct 6	Virgo
Nov 9	Libra
Dec 6	Scorpio
Dec 31	Sagittarius

1992

Jan 25	Capricorn
Feb 18	Aquarius
Mar 13	Pisces
Apr 7	Aries
May 1	Taurus
May 26	Gemini
Jun 19	Cancer
Jul 13	Leo
Aug 7	Virgo
Aug 21	Libra
Sep 25	Scorpio
Oct 19	Sagittarius
Nov 13	Capricorn
Dec 8	Aquarius

1993

Jan 3	Pisces
Feb 2	Aries
Jun 6	Taurus
Jul 6	Gemini
Aug 1	Cancer
Aug 27	Leo
Sep 21	Virgo
Oct 16	Libra
Nov 9	Scorpio
Dec 2	Sagittarius
Dec 26	Capricorn

1994

Jan 19	Aquarius
Feb 12	Pisces
Mar 8	Aries
Apr 1	Taurus
Apr 26	Gemini
May 21	Cancer
Jun 15	Leo
Jul 11	Virgo
Aug 7	Libra
Sep 7	Scorpio

1995

Jan 7	Sagittarius
Feb 4	Capricorn
Mar 2	Aquarius
Mar 28	Pisces
Apr 22	Aries
May 16	Taurus
Jun 10	Gemini
Jul 5	Cancer
Jul 29	Leo
Aug 23	Virgo
Sep 16	Libra
Oct 10	Scorpio
Nov 3	Sagittarius
Nov 27	Capricorn
Dec 21	Aquarius

1996

Jan 15	Pisces
Feb 9	Aries
Mar 6	Taurus
Apr 3	Gemini
Aug 7	Cancer
Sep 7	Leo
Oct 4	Virgo
Oct 29	Libra
Nov 23	Scorpio
Dec 17	Sagittarius

1997

10 Jan	Capricorn
Feb 3	Aquarius
Feb 27	Pisces
Mar 23	Aries
Apr 16	Taurus
May 10	Gemini
Jun 4	Cancer
Jun 28	Leo
Jul 23	Virgo
Aug 17	Libra
Sep 12	Scorpio

1997 (continued)

Oct 8	Sagittarius
Nov 5	Capricorn
Dec 12	Aquarius

1998

Jan 9	Capricorn
Mar 4	Aquarius
Apr 6	Pisces
May 3	Aries
May 29	Taurus
Jun 24	Gemini
Jul 19	Cancer
Aug 13	Leo
Sep 6	Virgo
Sep 30	Libra
Oct 24	Scorpio
Nov 17	Sagittarius
Dec 11	Capricorn

1999

Jan 4	Aquarius
Jan 28	Pisces
Feb 21	Aries
Mar 18	Taurus
Apr 12	Gemini
May 8	Cancer
Jun 5	Leo
Jul 12	Virgo
Aug 15	Leo
Oct 7	Virgo
Nov 9	Libra
Dec 5	Scorpio
Dec 31	Sagittarius

2000

Jan 24	Capricorn
Feb 18	Aquarius
Mar 13	Pisces
Apr 6	Aries
May 1	Taurus
May 15	Gemini
Jun 18	Cancer
Jul 13	Leo
Aug 6	Virgo
Aug 31	Libra
Sep 24	Scorpio
Oct 19	Sagittarius
Nov 13	Capricorn
Dec 8	Aquarius

2001

Jan 4	Pisces
Feb 3	Aries
Jun 7	Taurus
Jul 6	Gemini
Aug 2	Cancer
Aug 27	Leo
Sep 22	Virgo
Oct 16	Libra
Nov 9	Scorpio
Dec 3	Sagittarius
Dec 27	Capricorn

2002

Jan 20	Aquarius
Feb 13	Pisces
Mar 9	Aries
Apr 2	Taurus
Apr 26	Gemini
May 20	Cancer
Jun 15	Leo
Jul 11	Virgo
Aug 8	Libra
Sep 9	Scorpio

2003

Jan 8	Sagittarius
Feb 5	Capricorn
Mar 3	Aquarius
Mar 28	Pisces
Apr 22	Aries
May 17	Taurus
Jun 11	Gemini
Jul 5	Cancer
Jul 30	Leo
Aug 23	Virgo
Sep 16	Libra
Oct 10	Scorpio
Nov 3	Sagittarius
Nov 28	Capricorn
Dec 22	Aquarius

2004

Jan 15	Pisces
Feb 9	Aries
Mar 6	Taurus
Apr 4	Gemini
Aug 8	Cancer
Sep 7	Leo
Oct 4	Virgo
Oct 30	Libra
Nov 23	Scorpio
Dec 17	Sagittarius

2005

Jan 10	Capricorn
Feb 3	Aquarius
Feb 27	Pisces
Mar 24	Aries
Apr 16	Taurus
May 11	Gemini
Jun 4	Cancer
Jun 29	Leo
Jul 24	Virgo
Aug 18	Libra
Sep 12	Scorpio
Oct 9	Sagittarius
Nov 6	Capricorn
Dec 16	Aquarius

2006

Jan 2	Capricorn
Mar 6	Aquarius
Apr 7	Pisces
May 3	Aries
May 30	Taurus
Jun 25	Gemini
Jul 20	Cancer
Aug 13	Leo
Sep 7	Virgo
Oct 1	Libra
Oct 25	Scorpio
Nov 18	Sagittarius
Dec 12	Capricorn

2007

Jan 4	Aquarius
Jan 29	Pisces
Feb 22	Aries
Mar 18	Taurus
Apr 13	Gemini
May 9	Cancer
Jun 6	Leo
Jul 15	Virgo
Aug 10	Leo
Oct 9	Virgo
Nov 9	Libra
Dec 6	Scorpio
Dec 31	Sagittarius

2008

Jan 26	Capricorn
Feb 18	Aquarius
Mar 14	Pisces
Apr 7	Aries
May 1	Taurus
May 25	Gemini
Jun 19	Cancer
Jul 13	Leo
Aug 7	Virgo
Aug 31	Libra
Sep 26	Scorpio
Oct 19	Sagittarius
Nov 13	Capricorn
Dec 8	Aquarius

2009

Jan 4	Pisces
Feb 4	Aries
Apr 12	Pisces
Apr 25	Aries
Jun 7	Taurus
Jul 6	Gemini
Aug 2	Cancer
Aug 27	Leo
Sep 21	Virgo
Oct 15	Libra
Nov 9	Scorpio
Dec 2	Sagittarius
Dec 26	Capricorn

2010

Jan 19	Aquarius
Feb 12	Pisces
Mar 8	Aries
Apr 1	Taurus
Apr 26	Gemini
May 21	Cancer
Jun 15	Leo
Jul 11	Virgo
Aug 8	Libra
Sep 9	Scorpio
Nov 9	Libra
Dec 1	Scorpio

Mars in the signs and houses

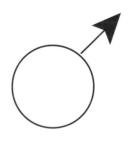 Mars provides a powerful masculine energy to the horoscope. It denotes passion, vitality, sexuality, competitiveness, and an inner drive that can be used in a positive or a negative fashion. The red planet is traditionally associated with war but also with sports, competition in general and other "masculine" pursuits, such as need for speed that can be found in motor racing.

Mars in Aries and the first house

Mars is the planet that rules the sign of Aries and when it is found here it is referred to as being "dignified." People who are born with Mars in this position usually possess a powerful physical presence. They also have enormous reserves of energy and are highly sexed. They need an outlet for their boundless energy and constant relief from boredom. Action is vastly preferred to words ,and new challenges are frequently sought. A natural leader, interested in competitive activities, Martial Ariens are difficult people to beat.

Mars in Taurus and the second house

Practicality is a Martial Taurean's main advantage. Naturally honest, this type may sometimes be extremely tactless. Those with Mars in Taurus naturally like routine and hate sudden change. The earthy nature of Taurus combined with the energy of Mars ensures that the Martial Taureans are very passionate, although he can also be extremely possessive. This is not a person who will accept that he or she has any limitations at all. Workaholic tendencies can result in a burn-out unless a gentler more accepting attitude is adopted.

Mars in Gemini and the third house

People with Mars in Gemini are often witty, talkative, and extremely charming, yet their nervous, restless energy makes them difficult to live with. The Martial Gemini has a low boredom threshold and is involved in a constant search for something (or someone) to occupy his interest. This sometimes involves leaving behind an unfinished project or a familiar face simply because the job or indeed the person has failed to hold the Martial Gemini's attention.

Mars in Cancer or the fourth house

Mars is in "fall" in Cancer and therefore not so aggressive. Very attached to home and family, this type is far more gentle than other Martial characters. However, this is not to say that there is no rage, it is just that it is expressed within the domestic environment rather than without. Affections are very strong, however, and there is a profound instinctive need to relate to loved ones on the deepest level. Metalwork, carpentry, and machinery might appeal as an outlet for frustrated energies.

People with Mars in Leo or the fifth house are great exponents of the "hard sell" and make formidable salesmen.

Mars in Leo or the fifth house

The energies of Mars find a fulfilling outlet when the planet is in this sign or house. Very competitive, this robust type enjoys sports and physical challenges. Often pushy, they can be excellent salespersons because they will wear the opposition down. Equally pushy with their children because they want their offspring to succeed in life. Having said that, they are very loving and protective to children. Additionally, Mars here indicates a high sex drive.

Mars in Virgo or the sixth house

This is a hard and conscientious worker when the job holds interest, but a shirker and a time-server when it does not. As a boss, this Martial type can be hard on subordinates, using eloquence to cutting effect, although there will also be moments of astonishing kindness. Intellectually keen, this type likes mental challenges and can be an excellent, impartial critic. Sexually they are firebrands, combining earthy sensuality with molten passion.

Those with Mars in Cancer or the fourth house relate to their loved ones on the deepest level.

Mars in Libra or the seventh house

Mars is considered to be in "detriment" in Libra, causing high hopes in partnership issues to be dashed. There seems to be an emotional need to relate to someone special, but an equally pressing desire for self-reliance. Consequently, there could be problematic commitment issues in this person's life. There may also be a quarrelsome tendency that vies with the sexual side of a relationship for ascendancy.

The aggressive nature of Mars is often channeled into fields such as engineering when it is found in Scorpio or the eighth house.

Mars in Scorpio or the eighth house

Traditionally, Mars was considered the ruler of Scorpio (although this is now shared with Pluto). The planet is strong here and the aggressive nature is often channeled into fields such as mining, sewer work, butchery, dentistry, surgery, or engineering—all of which involve delving deeply into something. These people are great strategists, are often sexy, pretty possessive, and can be guilty about their indiscretions. There may be a dark or morbid side to their natures.

Mars in Sagittarius and the ninth house

Those with Mars in Sagittarius or the ninth house are great explorers and are fascinated by distant regions of the world.

Outgoing, dynamic, and adventurous, this Martial type is constantly on the go, and is the natural explorer of the zodiac. They love travel, often to distant and obscure regions. Highly sexed, often uncomfortably so, they are wild and free, with variable tastes. Commitment is obviously a problem here. This type is usually very intelligent too, often highly qualified, with an open mind and an eye for detail.

The Mars in Pisces or twelfth house type is often self-sacrificing, caring deeply for others.

Mars in Capricorn and the tenth house

When in Capricorn Mars is "exalted," so these people are very ambitious, single minded, and self-reliant. There is often an attraction to politics, the armed forces or engineering. They think big, and grand enterprises excite them even more than sex. On the other hand, their sexual life can be a competitive arena in its own right, so striving for achievement here could also be a major factor.

Mars in Aquarius and the eleventh house

This type of person is a good friend but a bad enemy. Convivial and outgoing, this Martial person will make friends very easily, but can equally quickly fall out with them and make new ones. They are natural politicians, but not in the least diplomatic. Often attracted to causes rather than people, their sex lives are therefore unstable. Sometimes they are very sexy, and at other times show not the slightest inclination.

Mars in Pisces and the twelfth house

This is the most caring type of Martial personality. Self-sacrificing for friends and family, they care deeply for others and would rather bear pain themselves than see it inflicted on anyone else. This type has an inner strength, even though they may appear to be shy and introverted. Most embark on an inner spiritual quest at some time in their lives. The cause of this is usually a deep-seated anger that they are unable to express, or feelings of love that they feel have to be kept hidden.

Mars in Capricorn or the tenth house makes a person extremely competitive.

Mars calendar 1950-2010

1950
Jan 1	Libra
Mar 28	Virgo
Jun 11	Libra
Aug 10	Scorpio
Sep 25	Sagittarius
Nov 6	Capricorn
Dec 15	Aquarius

1951
Jan 22	Pisces
Mar 1	Aries
Apr 10	Taurus
May 21	Gemini
Jul 3	Cancer
Aug 18	Leo
Oct 5	Virgo
Nov 24	Libra

1952
Jan 20	Scorpio
Aug 27	Sagittarius
Oct 12	Capricorn
Nov 21	Aquarius
Dec 30	Pisces

1953
Feb 8	Aries
Mar 20	Taurus
May 1	Gemini
Jun 14	Cancer
Jul 29	Leo
Sep 14	Virgo
Nov 1	Libra
Dec 20	Scorpio

1954
Feb 9	Sagittarius
Apr 12	Capricorn
Jul 3	Sagittarius
Aug 24	Capricorn
Oct 21	Aquarius
Dec 4	Pisces

1955
Jan 15	Aries
Feb 26	Taurus
Apr 10	Gemini
May 26	Cancer
Jul 11	Leo
Aug 27	Virgo
Oct 13	Libra
Nov 29	Scorpio

1956
Jan 14	Sagittarius
Feb 28	Capricorn
Apr 14	Aquarius
Jun 3	Pisces
Dec 6	Aries

1957
Jan 28	Taurus
Mar 17	Gemini
May 4	Cancer
Jun 21	Leo
Aug 8	Virgo
Sep 24	Libra
Nov 8	Scorpio
Dec 23	Sagittarius

1958
Feb 3	Capricorn
Mar 17	Aquarius
Apr 27	Pisces
Jun 7	Aries
Jul 21	Taurus
Sep 21	Gemini
Oct 29	Taurus

1959
Feb 10	Gemini
Apr 10	Cancer
Jul 1	Leo
Jul 20	Virgo
Sep 5	Libra
Oct 21	Scorpio
Dec 3	Sagittarius

1960
Jan 14	Capricorn
Feb 23	Aquarius
Apr 2	Pisces
May 11	Aries
Jun 20	Taurus
Aug 2	Gemini
Sep 21	Cancer

1961
Feb 5	Gemini
Feb 7	Cancer
May 6	Leo
Jun 28	Virgo
Aug 17	Libra
Oct 1	Scorpio
Nov 13	Sagittarius
Dec 24	Capricorn

1962
Feb 1	Aquarius
Mar 12	Pisces
Apr 19	Aries
May 28	Taurus
Jul 9	Gemini
Aug 22	Cancer
Oct 11	Leo

1963
Jun 3	Virgo
Jul 27	Libra
Sep 12	Scorpio
Oct 25	Sagittarius
Dec 5	Capricorn

1964
Jan 13	Aquarius
Feb 20	Pisces
Mar 29	Aries
May 7	Taurus
Jun 17	Gemini
Jul 30	Cancer
Sep 15	Leo
Nov 6	Virgo

1965
Jun 29 — Libra
Aug 20 — Scorpio
Oct 4 — Sagittarius
Nov 14 — Capricorn
Dec 23 — Aquarius

1966
Jan 30 — Pisces
Mar 9 — Aries
Apr 17 — Taurus
May 28 — Gemini
Jul 11 — Cancer
Aug 25 — Leo
Oct 12 — Virgo
Dec 4 — Libra

1967
Feb 12 — Scorpio
Mar 31 — Libra
Jul 19 — Scorpio
Sep 10 — Sagittarius
Oct 23 — Capricorn
Dec 1 — Aquarius

1968
Jan 9 — Pisces
Feb 17 — Aries
Mar 27 — Taurus
May 8 — Gemini
Jun 21 — Cancer
Aug 5 — Leo
Sep 21 — Virgo
Nov 9 — Libra
Dec 29 — Scorpio

1969
Feb 25 — Sagittarius
Sep 21 — Capricorn
Nov 4 — Aquarius
Dec 15 — Pisces

1970
Jan 24 — Aries
Mar 7 — Taurus
Apr 18 — Gemini
Jun 2 — Cancer
Jul 18 — Leo
Sep 3 — Virgo
Oct 20 — Libra
Dec 6 — Scorpio

1971
Jan 23 — Sagittarius
Mar 12 — Capricorn
May 3 — Aquarius
Nov 6 — Pisces
Dec 26 — Aries

1972
Feb 10 — Taurus
Mar 27 — Gemini
May 12 — Cancer
Jun 28 — Leo
Aug 15 — Virgo
Sep 30 — Libra
Nov 15 — Scorpio
Dec 30 — Sagittarius

1973
Feb 12 — Capricorn
Mar 26 — Aquarius
May 8 — Pisces
Jun 20 — Aries
Aug 12 — Taurus
Oct 29 — Aries
Dec 24 — Taurus

1974
Feb 27 — Gemini
Apr 20 — Cancer
Jun 9 — Leo
Jul 27 — Virgo
Sep 12 — Libra
Oct 28 — Scorpio
Dec 10 — Sagittarius

1975
Jan 21 — Capricorn
Mar 3 — Aquarius
Apr 11 — Pisces
May 21 — Aries
Jul 1 — Taurus
Aug 14 — Gemini
Oct 17 — Cancer
Nov 25 — Gemini

1976
Mar 18 — Cancer
May 16 — Leo
Jul 6 — Virgo
Aug 24 — Libra
Oct 8 — Scorpio
Nov 20 — Sagittarius

1977
Jan 1 — Capricorn
Feb 9 — Aquarius
Mar 20 — Pisces
Apr 27 — Aries
Jun 6 — Taurus
Jul 17 — Gemini
Sep 1 — Cancer
Oct 26 — Leo

1978
26 Jan — Cancer
Apr 10 — Leo
Jun 14 — Virgo
Aug 4 — Libra
Sep 19 — Scorpio
Nov 2 — Sagittarius
Dec 12 — Capricorn

1979
Jan 20 — Aquarius
Feb 27 — Pisces
Apr 7 — Aries
May 16 — Taurus
Jun 26 — Gemini
Aug 8 — Cancer
Sep 24 — Leo
Nov 19 — Virgo

1980
Mar 11	Leo
May 4	Virgo
Jul 10	Libra
Aug 29	Scorpio
Oct 12	Sagittarius
Nov 22	Capricorn
Dec 30	Aquarius

1981
Feb 6	Pisces
Mar 17	Aries
Apr 25	Taurus
Jun 5	Gemini
Jul 18	Cancer
Sep 2	Leo
Oct 21	Virgo
Dec 16	Libra

1982
Aug 3	Scorpio
Sep 20	Sagittarius
Oct 31	Capricorn
Dec 10	Aquarius

1983
Jan 17	Pisces
Feb 25	Aries
Apr 5	Taurus
May 16	Gemini
Jun 29	Cancer
Aug 13	Leo
Sep 30	Virgo
Nov 18	Libra

1984
Jan 11	Scorpio
Aug 17	Sagittarius
Oct 5	Capricorn
Nov 15	Aquarius
Dec 25	Pisces

1985
Feb 2	Aries
Mar 15	Taurus
Apr 26	Gemini
Jun 9	Cancer
Jul 5	Leo
Sep 10	Virgo
Oct 27	Libra
Dec 14	Scorpio

1986
Feb 2	Sagittarius
Mar 28	Capricorn
Oct 9	Aquarius
Nov 26	Pisces

1987
Jan 8	Aries
Feb 20	Taurus
Apr 5	Gemini
May 21	Cancer
Jul 6	Leo
Aug 22	Virgo
Oct 8	Libra
Nov 24	Scorpio

1988
Jan 8	Sagittarius
Feb 22	Capricorn
Apr 6	Aquarius
May 22	Pisces
Jul 13	Aries
Oct 23	Pisces
Nov 1	Aries

1989
Jan 19	Taurus
Mar 11	Gemini
Apr 29	Cancer
Jun 16	Leo
Aug 3	Virgo
Sep 19	Libra
Nov 4	Scorpio
Dec 18	Sagittarius

1990
Jan 29	Capricorn
Mar 11	Aquarius
Apr 20	Pisces
May 31	Aries
Jul 12	Taurus
Aug 31	Gemini
Dec 14	Taurus

1991
Jan 21	Gemini
Apr 3	Cancer
May 26	Leo
Jul 15	Virgo
Oct 16	Scorpio
Nov 29	Sagittarius

1992
Jan 9	Capricorn
Feb 18	Aquarius
Mar 28	Pisces
May 5	Aries
Jun 14	Taurus
Jul 26	Gemini
Sep 12	Cancer

1993
Apr 27	Leo
Jun 23	Virgo
Aug 12	Libra
Sep 27	Scorpio
Nov 9	Sagittarius
Dec 20	Capricorn

1994
Jan 28	Aquarius
Mar 7	Pisces
Apr 14	Aries
May 23	Taurus
Jul 3	Gemini
Aug 16	Cancer
Oct 4	Leo
Dec 12	Virgo

1995

Jan 22	Leo
May 25	Virgo
Jul 21	Libra
Sep 7	Scorpio
Oct 20	Sagittarius
Nov 30	Capricorn

1996

Jan 8	Aquarius
Feb 15	Pisces
Mar 24	Aries
May 2	Taurus
Jun 12	Gemini
Jul 25	Cancer
Sep 9	Leo
Oct 30	Virgo

1997

Jan 3	Libra
Mar 8	Virgo
Jun 19	Libra
Aug 14	Scorpio
Sep 28	Sagittarius
Nov 9	Capricorn
Dec 18	Aquarius

1998

Jan 25	Pisces
Mar 4	Aries
Apr 13	Taurus
May 24	Gemini
Jul 6	Cancer
Aug 20	Leo
Oct 7	Virgo
Nov 27	Libra

1999

Jan 26	Scorpio
May 5	Libra
Jul 5	Scorpio
Sep 2	Sagittarius
Oct 17	Capricorn
Nov 26	Aquarius

2000

Jan 4	Pisces
Feb 12	Aries
Mar 23	Taurus
May 3	Gemini
Jun 16	Cancer
Aug 1	Leo
Sep 17	Virgo
Nov 4	Libra
Dec 23	Scorpio

2001

Feb 15	Sagittarius
Sep 9	Capricorn
Oct 28	Aquarius
Dec 9	Pisces

2002

Jan 19	Aries
Mar 2	Taurus
Apr 14	Gemini
May 29	Cancer
Jul 14	Leo
Aug 30	Virgo
Oct 15	Libra
Dec 2	Scorpio

2003

Jan 18	Sagittarius
Mar 5	Capricorn
Apr 22	Aquarius
Jun 17	Pisces
Dec 17	Aries

2004

eb 4 F	Taurus
Mar 22	Gemini
May 8	Cancer
Jun 23	Leo
Aug 11	Virgo
Sep 27	Libra
Nov 12	Scorpio
Dec 26	Sagittarius

2005

Feb 7	Capricorn
Mar 21	Aquarius
May 2	Pisces
Jun 13	Aries
Jul 29	Taurus

2006

Feb 18	Gemini
Apr 15	Cancer
Jun 4	Leo
Jul 23	Virgo
Sep 9	Libra
Oct 24	Scorpio
Dec 7	Sagittarius

2007

Jan 17	Capricorn
Feb 27	Aquarius
Apr 7	Pisces
May 16	Aries
Jun 25	Taurus
Aug 8	Gemini
Sep 29	Cancer

2008

Jan 1	Gemini
Mar 5	Cancer
May 10	Leo
Jul 2	Virgo
Aug 20	Libra
Oct 5	Scorpio
Nov 17	Sagittarius
Dec 28	Capricorn

2009

Feb 5	Aquarius
Mar 16	Pisces
Apr 23	Aries
Jun 1	Taurus
Jul 13	Gemini
Aug 26	Cancer
Oct 17	Leo

2010

Jun 8	Virgo
Jul 30	Libra
Sep 15	Scorpio
Oct 29	Sagittarius
Dec 8	Capricorn

Jupiter in the signs and houses

4

The sign that Jupiter was in at the time of your birth will throw considerable light on your beliefs and your value system. It also determines how adventurous you are and the way you attempt to expand your horizons throughout your life. Jupiter in some signs inclines the person to be a gambler or risk-taker, and in others it breathes life into what otherwise might be a dull personality. Jupiter is a wonderful indicator of where and how you are likely to find luck.

To analyse your own luck quotient, look through the list of dates on pages 106–107 to discover the dates of Jupiter's entry into each sign. Like all the planets, Jupiter travels in retrograde motion from time to time when it appears to travel backwards. Sometimes this happens within a single sign, but at other times, Jupiter moves into a new sign and then returns to the previous one for a while before moving on again. The dates for all these sign changes from the middle of the 20th century onward are given in the following table. Once you have looked at your luck quotient at birth, perhaps you would like to see how your luck will be during the next few years.

Jupiter in Aries or the first house

Broad-minded and cheerful, these subjects may be lucky in life, either making money easily or attaching themselves to partners who become rich. Attracted to the Jupiterian pursuits of travel, education, publishing, broadcasting, religion, or the law.

They learn a great deal about whatever is represented by the sign that this planet occupies. For example, Jupiter in the first house in Scorpio could bring an interest in forensic or medical matters.

With a nice smile, a friendly manner, they enjoy a happy-go-lucky outlook on life.

Land, farming, and animal husbandry are associated with Jupiter in Taurus or the second house.

Jupiter in Taurus or the second house

Lucky with money and possessions, these subjects could make money easily but they may be too generous or open-handed to keep it. They can earn money by dealing with foreigners or foreign goods. Land, farming, animal husbandry, or some other form of outdoor life can feature in these folks' lives.

The giant planet Jupiter encourages educational matters and a broad mind.

Jupiter in Gemini or the third house

(Jupiter is in "detriment" in Gemini and can promote flippancy)

These subjects get on well with their brothers and sisters. They are quite studious and may do well academically, either at school or later in life. They have a deep interest in communications and they may write or communicate for a living. Travel and foreigners are liked and may play a large part in these people's lives.

Jupiter in Cancer or the fourth house

(Jupiter is "exalted" in Cancer and therefore more optimistic and generous.)

Good relationships with parents and a good home life characterize this placement. Individuals may move house often or may make money out of property matters. Some inherit property, while others win a share in property through the courts. They can lack perspective or be too closely focused on home or family matters. Some work from their homes in some way.

Jupiter in Cancer or the fourth house is beneficial to property interests. Some with this placement inherit or win a legal right to a house. Others tend to move home often.

Jupiter in Leo or the fifth house

All forms of speculation are lucky for these subjects, and they are good at sports, and the creative arts. They may make money from sports, art, or some kind of glamor business. They may enjoy working with children or teaching them. They are religious or spiritual and they may teach in a Sunday school. These subjects may have a dramatic, larger-than-life manner, and they may be restless and easily bored. Their children do well and can have lucky lives in their turn.

Those with Jupiter in Leo or the fifth house often love sports and may make money from gambling and speculation.

Jupiter in Virgo or the sixth house

These subjects are happy at work and enjoy what they do. They make money from working and they could inherit a business. They may work in any of the Jupiterian professions, such as travel, the law, education, and religion. Travel interests them, and they are fond of animals. Hips and thighs may be weak or they may be prone to accidents if other factors on the chart point to this.

The hips and thighs provide potential health problems for those with Jupiter in the sixth house.

Jupiter in Libra or the seventh house

This is an excellent placement for partnerships, both of the working and the personal kind. Marriage may be either very good or very bad. These subjects are friendly and flirtatious, and they are especially attracted to foreigners or anyone who is different in some way. They are pleasant and patient personalities.

Those with Jupiter in Libra or the seventh house are very open, friendly, and, as adults can be quite flirtatious.

Jupiter in Scorpio or the eighth house

There is a strong chance that these subjects could inherit money. There may be a particularly easy or casual attitude towards death and the afterlife. These subjects may do very well from marriage and they could be attracted to partners from other countries or who are different in some way.

People with Jupiter in Scorpio or the eighth house often express a strangely casual attitude to death and the afterlife.

Jupiter in Sagittarius or the ninth house

(Jupiter is very strong here, being the ruler of Sagittarius.) All the Jupiterian interests are heightened with this placement, which means that these subjects may travel a lot, or be interested in religious, or spiritual matters. They may teach or work in the law, publishing or the media. These people are happy, lucky and sometimes reckless. They can be outspoken, eccentric or tactless. Their hips and thighs may be weak .

Jupiter rules Sagittarius so an astonishing love of travel is only to be expected if the planet is found there.

Jupiter in Capricorn or the tenth house

(Jupiter is in "fall" in Capricorn and can encourage black moods.) These subjects can do very well in their chosen career, and many achieve public acclaim. They have a good manner in business or politics, and they can be successful without making a great deal of effort. They usually make good money as well. They may have a rather dramatic personality, and they need variety in their working lives. They want to leave the world a better and happier place than when they found it.

People with Jupiter in Capricorn are often dramatic and love to make an impact.

Jupiter in Aquarius or the eleventh house

These subjects have many friends and acquaintances, some of them being rich or influential. They may have a strangely casual or pompous, high-minded attitude to others. They may embrace causes and they may use their wealth for philanthropy.

Those with Jupiter in Aquarius or the eleventh house are kind although they may be rather pompous.

Jupiter in Pisces or the twelfth house

These people prefer to work alone and they may achieve success in something like poetry, art, or dancing. They like the sea and are keen on travel. These subjects are also interested in medicine, especially the alternative variety. They are talented and musical, but gentle and shy when they are not on show

People with Jupiter in Pisces often find inner peace near to the sea.

Jupiter calendar 1950-2010

Starts 1950	Aquarius	Jun 10, 1960	Sagittarius	Jan 14, 1971	Sagittarius
Apr 15, 1950	Pisces	Oct 26, 1960	Capricorn	Jun 5, 1971	Scorpio
Sep 15, 1950	Aquarius	Nov 4, 1961	Aquarius	Sep 12, 1971	Sagittarius
Dec 2, 1950	Pisces	Mar 26, 1962	Pisces	Feb 7, 1972	Capricorn
Apr 22, 1951	Aries	Apr4, 1963	Aries	Jul 25, 1972	Sagittarius
Apr 29, 1952	Taurus	Apr 12, 1964	Taurus	Sep 26, 1972	Capricorn
May 10, 1953	Gemini	Apr 23, 1965	Gemini	Feb 23, 1973	Aquarius
May 24, 1954	Cancer	Sep 21, 1965	Cancer	Mar 8, 1974	Pisces
Jun 13, 1955	Leo	Nov 12, 1965	Gemini	Mar 19, 1975	Aries
Nov 17, 1955	Virgo	May6, 1966	Cancer	Mar 26, 1976	Taurus
Jan 18, 1956	Leo	28 Sep, 1966	Leo	Aug 28, 1976	Gemini
Jul 8, 1956	Virgo	16 Jan, 1967	Cancer	Oct 17, 1976	Taurus
Dec 12, 1956	Libra	May 23, 1967	Leo	Apr 4, 1977	Gemini
Feb 20, 1957	Virgo	Oct 19, 1967	Virgo	Aug 21, 1977	Cancer
Aug 6, 1957	Libra	Feb 27, 1968	Leo	Dec 31, 1977	Gemini
Jan 14, 1958	Scorpio	Jun 16, 1968	Virgo	Apr 12, 1978	Cancer
Mar 21, 1958	Libra	Nov 16, 1968	Libra	Sep 5, 1978	Leo
Sep 7, 1958	Scorpio	Mar 31, 1969	Virgo	Mar 1, 1979	Cancer
Feb 11, 1959	Sagittarius	Jul 16, 1969	Libra	Apr 20, 1979	Leo
Apr 25, 1959	Scorpio	Nov 17, 1979	Scorpio	Sep 29, 1979	Virgo
Oct 6, 1959	Sagittarius	Apr 29, 1970	Libra	Oct 27, 1980	Libra
Mar 2, 1960	Capricorn	Aug 16, 1970	Scorpio	Nov 27, 1981	Scorpio

Dec 26, 1982	Sagittarius	Jun 30, 2000	Gemini
Jan 20, 1984	Capricorn	Jul 14, 2001	Cancer
Feb 7, 1985	Aquarius	Aug 2, 2002	Leo
Feb 21, 1986	Pisces	Aug 28, 2003	Virgo
Mar 3, 1987	Aries	Sep 26, 2004	Libra
Mar 9, 1988	Taurus	Oct 27, 2005	Scorpio
Jul 22, 1988	Gemini	Nov 25, 2006	Sagittarius
Dec 1, 1988	Taurus	Dec 19, 2007	Capricorn
Mar 11, 1989	Gemini	Jan 5, 2009	Aquarius
Jul 31, 1989	Cancer	Jan 19, 2010	Pisces
Aug 18, 1990	Leo		
Sep 12, 1991	Virgo		
Oct 11, 1992	Libra		
Nov 10, 1993	Scorpio		
Dec 9, 1994	Sagittarius		
Jan 3, 1996	Capricorn		
Jan 22, 1997	Aquarius		
Feb 4, 1998	Pisces		
Feb 13, 1999	Aries		
Jun 28, 1999	Taurus		
Oct 23, 1999	Aries		
Oct 15, 2000	Taurus		

Saturn in the signs and houses

The zodiac sign in which Saturn is found has a direct bearing on our sense of purpose and life direction. Its influence is a very serious and sobering one because the ringed planet is not a bundle of laughs. In fact the planet has a very bad reputation in astrology. In the Middle Ages, Saturn was described as the "great malific" and was considered to be a harbinger of bad news. This point of view is unfair because, without the responsibility that Saturn conveys, we would not be able to deal with our own inhibitions and hang-ups.

Saturn is also called the great teacher and is the regulator of life. Its orbital period of approximately 29 years marks out the phases of our existence and is teaches us by our own experience. Sometimes the hard way! Although Jupiter brings optimism and wide horizons, without the dutiful influence of Saturn we could never cope with the setbacks that sometimes confront us.

Saturn in Aries or the first house can give rise to a serious, responsible personality.

Saturn in Aries or the first house

(Saturn is a gloomy influence in Aries, being in "fall.")
These subjects' parents may have had difficulty in conceiving them or giving birth. They may be conscious of having lived before and of not wanting to come back on this occasion! These people are inhibited, shy, and rather serious, but this may be covered up by an act of some kind. They take work and life seriously, and they take a responsible attitude to all that they do. They are often happier in old age, and their tendency to work hard pays off by giving them tremendous success and a very high income later in life. Strangely enough, Saturn on the ascendant (or in the fourth, seventh or tenth houses) can lead to fame and fortune.

Saturn in Taurus or the second house

These subjects work hard to make money and they succeed in due course. Success is hard-won but almost inevitable. They can be possessive and stingy.

Those with Saturn in Taurus work hard and are usually rewarded.

Saturn in Gemini individuals are often helpful toward their siblings.

Saturn in Gemini or the third house

Early life may be hard, with problems at school. Success and self-education come later, through these subjects' own efforts. They help their brothers and sisters, and have formal but good relations with their neighbors.

Saturn in Cancer or the fourth house

(Saturn is in "detriment" in Cancer and therefore indicates a difficult early life.) Saturn in Cancer indicates an unhappy and deprived early life, possibly with restrictive parents who may have been stingy and cruel. These subjects work hard to obtain a good family and home of their own, and they value these things when they have them. Their early problems may not have been due to bad parenting but to poverty or tribulation in the family (see also Saturn in Aries or the first house).

Saturn in Cancer or the fourth house individuals may experience an unhappy childhood.

Saturn in Leo or the fifth house

These subjects may have a domineering parent, usually the father. They may lack joy, or they may work too hard and forget how to play. Alternatively, they may take a serious attitude to creative endeavors and make a great success out of them. Children may be seen as a burden or, conversely, be much loved and very successful in their turn. Some people with this placement choose not to have children, or they may have difficulty in producing children.

Those with Saturn in Leo or the fifth house often have a domineering parent.

Saturn in Virgo or the sixth house

These subjects are hard workers with a serious attitude to their jobs, but they may not enjoy the work that they do. They may suffer from backaches. Although this house is not concerned with children, I have found that Saturn placed here can bring difficulties in either having children or bringing them up.

Saturn in Virgo or the sixth house types work hard, but frequently do not enjoy the jobs they choose.

Saturn in Libra subjects may marry late in life.

Saturn in Libra or the seventh house

(A mature influence prevails when Saturn is in Libra because it is "exalted.")

These people may marry late and to someone who is much older or much younger than themselves. There may be restriction or frustration in marriage, or as a result of marriage or business partnerships. They are faithful partners with a serious attitude to the partnership (see Saturn in Aries or the first house).

Saturn in Scorpio or the eighth house

A careful, responsible attitude to money, especially when dealing with other people's resources. It is possible that these subjects are somewhat sexually inhibited due to an overly strong moral code. They will possess a serious attitude to death and concepts of the afterlife, and will instinctively understand that everything is transitory.

Saturn in Scorpio or the eighth house can give rise to a serious attitude to death and the afterlife.

Saturn in Sagittarius or the ninth house

Deep thinkers who are dedicated to causes that can benefit mankind. These people are happier when they get older. Long-distance travel and foreigners may bring them problems, but alternatively, this could lead to an increase in status or money. They may spend a lifetime searching for spiritual experiences or some meaning to their lives.

Those with Saturn in Sagittarius or the ninth house may find that they are happier later in life than in their early years.

Saturn in Capricorn or the tenth house

(Saturn rules the sign of Capricorn so is especially powerful here.) Possibly ambitious to the exclusion of social and family life, obligations can weigh heavily on these subjects. They are conscientious workers who may not be recognized or remunerated properly for what they do. A career switch in mid-life can lead to later success. They may achieve fame and fortune, only to be disgraced publicly later.

Saturn in Capricorn or the tenth house types are hard workers, but may not receive the remuneration or recognition they deserve.

Those subjects with Saturn in Aquarius or the eleventh house may find that elderly relatives and friends come to their assistance.

Saturn in Aquarius or the eleventh house

(Saturn is almost as strong in Aquarius as it is in Capricorn.) These people take obligations to committees, causes, and groups of friends very seriously. They have influential friends who they use in order to get on. Alternatively, they may become so busy that they ignore their friends. Elderly relatives and friends may help them.

Saturn in Pisces or the twelfth house

This placement can lead to sadness and an inability to express oneself. They may be surrounded by relatives and still feel lonely. Some are their own worst enemies. Some turn their shyness and sensitivity to good account by taking up careers where they care for others. These people have a strong level of self-discipline.

Saturn in Pisces people frequently suffer from feelings of loneliness, even in a crowd.

Saturn calendar 1950-2010

Saturn spends about two years in each sign, so it is quiet easy to spot those years when it is working on your behalf or making life difficult for you. As with all the other planets, it does have periods of retrograde motion. The list below runs from the start of 1950 to 2010.

Starts 1950	Virgo	Sep 18, 1975	Leo	Oct 17, 2000	Taurus
Nov 21, 1950	Libra	Jan 15, 1976	Cancer	Apr 21, 2001	Gemini
Mar 8, 1951	Virgo	Jun 6, 1976	Leo	Jun 5, 2003	Cancer
Aug 14, 1951	Libra	Nov 18, 1977	Virgo	Jul 17, 2005	Leo
Oct 22, 1953	Scorpio	Jan 6, 1978	Leo	Sep 3, 2007	Virgo
Jan 13, 1956	Sagittarius	Jul 27, 1978	Virgo	Oct 30, 2009	Libra
May 15, 1956	Scorpio	Sep 22, 1980	Libra	Apr 8, 2010	Virgo
Oct 11, 1956	Sagittarius	Nov 30, 1982	Scorpio	Jul 22, 2010	Libra
Jan 6, 1959	Capricorn	May 7, 1983	Libra		
Jan 4, 1962	Aquarius	Aug 25, 1983	Scorpio		
Mar 25, 1964	Pisces	Nov 18, 1985	Sagittarius		
Sep 17, 1964	Aquarius	Feb 14, 1988	Capricorn		
Dec 17, 1964	Pisces	Jun 11, 1988	Sagittarius		
Mar 4, 1967	Aries	Nov 13, 1988	Capricorn		
Apr 30, 1969	Taurus	Feb 7, 1991	Aquarius		
19 Jun, 1971	Gemini	Jan 29, 1994	Pisces		
11 Jan, 1972	Taurus	Aug 8, 1996	Aries		
22 Feb, 1972	Gemini	Jun 10, 1998	Taurus		
2 Aug, 1973	Cancer	Oct 26, 1998	Aries		
8 Jan, 1974	Gemini	Mar 2, 1999	Taurus		
19 Apr, 1974	Cancer	Aug 11, 2000	Gemini		

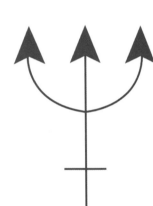

The distant planets in the houses

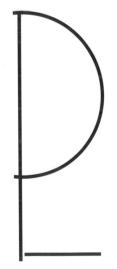

The remote planets Uranus, Neptune, and Pluto literally take years to move from one zodiac sign to another, so it is not necessary to interpret their zodiac positions. The placement of these planets in the zodiac will affect whole generations, rather than individuals. So, for a personal reading using these planets, we need only to refer to houses which they happen to occupy in your personal birth chart.

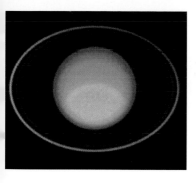

Uranus in the houses

URANUS IN THE FIRST HOUSE

Intelligent, unpredictable, individualistic, these people should have modern, scientific minds, but equally, may have unusual ideas or an unconventional lifestyle. They may be quite nervy or possibly have circulation problems. Friends will be extremely important to them.

URANUS IN THE SECOND HOUSE

These subjects may have gains and losses on a grand scale, resulting in an unpredictable income that may come from two or more different sources. Possessions, resources, or jobs may suddenly appear and disappear just as quickly; fortunately they have a non-materialist attitude to life. Friends may help these subjects to find something that they treasure, but their values would be unusual in any case.

URANUS IN THE THIRD HOUSE

With a lively, intelligent mind and unusual ideas, these individuals may experience frequent changes of school and/or an unusual education. Odd experiences, or an unusual attitude to brothers and sisters may lead them to become close to friends who they then treat like siblings. Friends and people who are Aquarians will tend to encourage and educate these subjects.

URANUS IN THE FOURTH HOUSE

An unstable situation early in life my cause many upheavals or changes of home. They may have been disruptive and odd children, and so choose to live in an unusual home or under strange circumstances later in life. They might make their home with a friend.

The unusual creativity of Uranus in the fifth house individuals may lead them to become inventors.

Uranus in the sixth house individuals can be liable to sudden ailments, particularly when stressed.

Uranus in the eighth house types may choose unusual types of employment

URANUS IN THE FIFTH HOUSE

Gifted and bright, these people might be inventors, and are certainly creative in an unusual way; they may chase after strange love affairs or peculiar sexual experiences. With uncommon pastimes or hobbies, they will have clever children. They will find inspiration in friends and may have casual love affairs with friends who become lovers and then slip back to being friends once again.

URANUS IN THE SIXTH HOUSE

Uranus in this position suggests unpredictability at work or individuals who hold down two jobs or perhaps a very unusual one. They may be prone to sudden unexplained ailments, especially when under stress. They are likely to have many friends, as well as close relationships with work colleagues.

URANUS IN THE SEVENTH HOUSE

These individuals must have mental rapport with any partner, and require an unusual and very free marriage. Bizarre and unlikely relationships are likely, both personally and in professional circumstance. They might choose to live with a friend and have sexual relationships away from the home.

URANUS IN THE EIGHTH HOUSE

They have the potential to gain and lose money from business partnerships or marriage circumstances and have unusual ideas in the realms of work, money, and sex. They may be morbid or obsessed by sex, perhaps attached to a strange or obsessive partner. They might have a curious attitude to friends.

URANUS IN THE NINTH HOUSE

Accident-prone and susceptible to mental stress, these types might spend a lot of time traveling and have great gains and losses as a result; they could be a lucky gamblers. Keen on helping groups of people to understand religion or spirituality, they make excellent clairvoyants or mediums. They could acquire friends through hobbies, interests, or while traveling.

URANUS IN THE TENTH HOUSE

Far-sighted, with leadership qualities, these subjects dislike routine and may undergo sudden changes in their career. They may have two jobs which are equally important, but very different from one another. Good friends will appear at work, or they will choose to work with groups of friends, generally working with or for groups of people. They regard education as a means to advance in life, and often like astrology.

URANUS IN THE ELEVENTH HOUSE

These subjects like societies, clubs, and group activities, and quickly gain many friends, although they often lose them just as quickly. They might be eccentric or different in some way. Far-sighted and broad-minded, these people never stop educating themselves, and may be keen astrologers.

URANUS IN THE TWELFTH HOUSE

These subjects may have terrific clairvoyant abilities and they may be keen on astrology. Secretive, they may harbor odd ideas and feelings and can be very spiritual and mystical. These people may hide their emotions, or they may be confused or upset by feelings of inner turmoil. Eccentric would be a mild description for this type.

Uranus in the eleventh house types can tend to be eccentric and broad-minded.

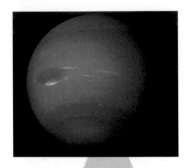

Neptune in the houses

NEPTUNE IN THE FIRST HOUSE

These subjects are dreamy, sensitive and artistic. They may be impractical, disorganized, chaotic, and forgetful. Some are eccentric, whereas others may be more conventional but drawn to mystical or artistic pursuits. They are often talented, musical or artistic, and some make excellent photographers.

NEPTUNE IN THE SECOND HOUSE

They may not be able to keep money for long, or are possibly mean and money-minded. However they are usually non-materialistic in outlook. Valuing kindness and caring for others, they may make money from mystical or other unusual interests. They may work successfully in something to do with liquids such as the oil industry, sailing, fishing, shipping, plumbing, etc. They are lovers of the esthetic and of artistic objects.

Those with Neptune in the second house may choose fishing, or something water-related, as their job.

NEPTUNE IN THE THIRD HOUSE

These subjects are intuitive and imaginative. They may lack concentration or they may have a wonderful gift of communication through visual effects (such as video or photography) or through descriptive writing. They could be some kind of therapist and are good actors, but may be something of a drifter.

NEPTUNE IN THE FOURTH HOUSE

These subjects may love their homes, but they may not keep them very tidy. Alternatively, the home could be a spotless place of great beauty. There should be a good relationship with the parents, with an intuitive, almost telepathic link. They may be disorganized in practical matters, but possess a strong imagination or inner life.

Those with Neptune in the fourth house might have immaculate surroundings, or they might be extremely untidy people.

NEPTUNE IN THE NINTH HOUSE

They are likely to be inspired to work in the field of philosophy or religion, or may do well in trades connected to the sea or to liquids, such as the oil industry, hairdressing, etc. They could travel a great deal and could fall in love while traveling. These subjects help people who are in trouble, or who cannot help themselves, and they have the potential be involved in unusual legal cases which go on for years.

For those with Neptune in the ninth house, religion might be a strong calling.

NEPTUNE IN THE TENTH HOUSE

These subjects may choose a career for idealistic reasons. They may work in feminine or creative fields such as photography, art, dancing, poetry, or something similar. Alternatively, they could choose nursing, working with prisoners, the mentally-handicapped, or some other form of caring occupation. They aspire to something greater than simply earning money and they want to heal the world. They may go through many changes in life, and they could be greatly helped or let down by others in career matters.

NEPTUNE IN THE ELEVENTH HOUSE

Idealistic, artistic and creative, these subjects may find it hard to get anything done at all. Their aims are intellectual and imaginative, and they are keen on groups who have the same kind of goal. They could be greatly helped or badly let down by friends. They may be mystical, intuitive, and interested in divination, feng shui, astrology, and a host of other mystical arts.

NEPTUNE IN THE TWELFTH HOUSE

Likely to be interested in poetry, ballet, culture, art, and music, these individuals could be great animal lovers or lovers of people, especially those who need help. Mystical, spiritual, and other-worldly, they may have great sadness in life or simply be drawn inward to a contemplative existence.

Neptune in the tenth house can bring with it a desire to work in healing in some form.

Pluto in the houses

Those with Pluto in the second house may have the potential to earn a lot of money.

Homes are of utmost importance to those with a fourth-house Pluto.

PLUTO IN THE FIRST HOUSE

These subjects have attractive, magnetic personalities and dynamic natures. They are attracted to big business or to positions of power and authority. Their lives go in distinct phases with gains and losses every few years. Can brood and have a terrible temper. They tend to control or rule others if they can.

PLUTO IN THE SECOND HOUSE

These subjects have a good grasp of business affairs and have the potential to make lots of money, although they may lose it on a grand scale too. They also have a deep need for security, and may see money and possessions as a form of this. They can be covetous and are likely to be hoarders.

PLUTO IN THE THIRD HOUSE

These subjects have terrific powers of concentration and they finish the projects that they start. They can be moody and depressed at times. They may do much to help their siblings or, alternatively, they can be unkind to them (sometimes at the same time). These people can make money by teaching and writing, and they enjoy influencing others via the medium of words.

PLUTO IN THE FOURTH HOUSE

These people feel very deeply about their homes, their parents, and their marriage partners. They may try to control or dominate their families and they may be too fond of their own point of view when in the home situation. They are likely to inherit property.

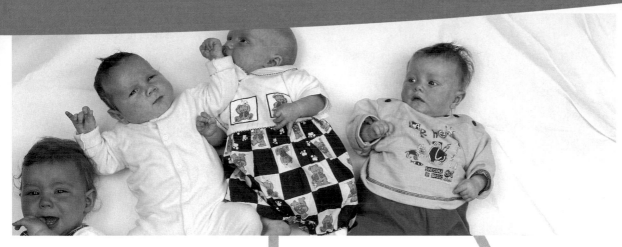

Children are a primary concern to individuals with Pluto in the fifth house.

PLUTO IN THE FIFTH HOUSE

Children are important to these subjects and they may go to a lot of trouble either to have children or to bring them up. They may live for pleasure or, alternatively, they may take a serious view of pastimes, sports and so on. These people enjoy the arts and music, and they could be drawn to gambling in order to make money. Some have many torrid love affairs, others put their energies into creative schemes.

PLUTO IN THE SIXTH HOUSE

These people try to reform or change their colleagues' working practises and may be very hard workers or simply be too concerned with working life. They may have weak health or irritable bowels, and some of these problems may be due to tension.

Those with Pluto in the eighth house can have a real gift for uncovering secrets.

PLUTO IN THE SEVENTH HOUSE

These people can make good business partners, possibly being a little overbearing. Similarly, they might be demanding marriage partners with too much emphasis on sex. Their feelings are intense, and jealousy is likely to be a problem, but these subjects may be on the receiving end of this kind of treatment, rather than dishing it out themselves. They may inherit possessions from a partner.

PLUTO IN THE EIGHTH HOUSE

Intuitive individuals, especially where money and business is concerned, they may inherit a legacy from a partner. They may work for the community or in a mediumistic or spiritual manner, and could be keen on typically Plutonic interests such as the afterlife, death, sex, birth, medical, forensic, or investigative matters. If so, they may work on the insides or the underneath of things, in trades such as butchery, mining, or simply digging out secrets. Analytical, logical, with searching minds, and very secretive natures, they could be great animal lovers.

Subjects with Pluto in the tenth house can have a tendency to be a little unbalanced.

Those with Pluto in the ninth house often love to travel.

PLUTO IN THE NINTH HOUSE

These people may be bound up with foreigners or distant places. They may force their religious or spiritual views on others, or they may drag others through the courts. They may be keen on educating themselves and others, and could be very fond of animals, or keen to travel to strange places.

PLUTO IN THE TENTH HOUSE

These subjects can reach great heights of influence, or they can attach themselves to influential people. They may work in fields where they can influence others or even take them over in some way. This is a good placement for hypnotists, anesthetists, and dream analysts, for instance. There may be powerful urges to rule, and these subjects may be obsessed with dreams of grandeur. They may be attracted to drugs, or may work with them. They are often dynamic, powerful, or somewhat unbalanced.

PLUTO IN THE ELEVENTH HOUSE

These people may be searching for the truth, and may choose psychology or astrology as a means of finding it. These subjects may have powerful and influential friends or, alternatively, they may try to influence groups of people or befriends people in order to change or influence them. Generally speaking, they are friendly, likeable, and fond of working for committees, clubs, and societies. They are likely to be well-balanced and sensible, although with one or two peculiar ideas from time to time.

PLUTO IN THE TWELFTH HOUSE

These subjects have hidden talents and interests. They may be drawn to hidden or taboo love affairs of some sort. They may have hidden problems of a psychological kind, such as suppressed anger, or hatred for something that has been done to them by others. They may strive to find some kind of mystical truth and then express this to others in the form of poetry or music.

The calendar of the distant planets

The last three planets, the most distant from the Sun, are Uranus, Neptune, and Pluto and their orbits are so slow that they affect whole segments of a person's life—indeed Neptune and Pluto can affect a whole generation. Here are the dates on which these three planets change sign from, 1950 to 2010.

Uranus		**Neptune**		**Pluto**	
Starts 1950	Cancer	Starts 1950	Libra	Starts 1950	Leo
Aug 25, 1955	Leo	Dec , 1955	Scorpio	Oct 21, 1956	Virgo
Jan 29, 1956	Cancer	Mar 13, 1956	Libra	Jan 16, 1957	Leo
Jun 11, 1956	Leo	Oct 20, 1956	Scorpio	Aug 20, 1957	Virgo
Nov 2, 1961	Virgo	Jan 5, 1970	Sagittarius	Oct 6, 1971	Libra
Jan 11, 1962	Leo	May 4, 1970	Scorpio	Apr 18, 1972	Virgo
Aug 11, 1962	Virgo	Nov 7, 1970	Sagittarius	Jul 31, 1972	Libra
Sep 29, 1968	Libra	Jan 20, 1984	Capricorn	Nov 6, 1983	Scorpio
May 21, 1969	Virgo	Jun 24, 1984	Sagittarius	May 19, 1984	Libra
Jun 25, 1969	Libra	Nov 22, 1984	Capricorn	Aug 29, 1984	Scorpio
Nov 22, 1974	Scorpio	Jan 30, 1998	Aquarius	Jan 18, 1995	Sagittarius
May 2, 1975	Libra	Aug 24, 1998	Capricorn	Apr 22, 1995	Scorpio
Sep 9, 1975	Scorpio	Nov 29, 1998	Aquarius	Nov 11, 1995	Sagittarius
Feb 18, 1981	Sagittarius			Jan 27, 2008	Capricorn
Mar 21, 1981	Scorpio			Jun 15, 2008	Sagittarius
Nov 17, 1981	Sagittarius			Nov 28, 2008	Capricorn
Feb 14, 1988	Capricorn				
May 28, 1988	Sagittarius				
Dec 3, 1988	Capricorn				
Apr 2, 1995	Aquarius				
Jun 10, 1995	Capricorn				
Jan 13, 1995	Aquarius				
Feb 11 2003	Pisces				
Sep 16 2003	Aquarius				
Dec 31 2003	Pisces				
May 29, 2010	Aries				
Aug 15, 2010	Pisces				

Planetary aspects

You now have sufficient information to draw up and interpret your own birth chart with enough details to keep you occupied for some time. However, anyone who has an inkling of the more difficult stuff in astrology will immediately realize that this is not the end of it. There is the question of aspects to consider. To put it simply, aspects are the relationships of the planets to each other, usually expressed as a number of degrees of the circle. Since we have carefully skirted over the subject of degrees in this book we'll only look at the zodiac signs that the planets occupy to get an idea of their inter-relationships.

Conjunction

Two planets in the same sign of the zodiac make a conjunction, and this is either an easy or a difficult thing to live with, depending upon the planets in question.

Sextile

Two planets that are two signs apart—harmonious and helpful.

Square

Two planets three signs apart—very difficult.

Trine

Two planets four signs apart—creative and pleasant.

Opposition

Two planets six signs apart (ie on opposite signs of the birth chart). This can be useful for relationship matters but otherwise difficult in more practical affairs.

There are more aspects than these, but these are the most important and most powerful aspects, and they are quite enough for a beginner to cope with.

Conclusion

By now you will have got all the information that you need to create a reasonably accurate birth chart for yourself, your family, and your friends. You will be familiar with the functions of the Sun, Moon, and rising signs in both the zodiac signs and the houses of the horoscope. As well as learning something about the characteristics and effects of the inner planets, Mercury, Venus, Mars, Jupiter, and Saturn, plus the more long-term effects of those cold, distant outer planets Uranus, Neptune, and Pluto. However, this is not the end of the story or indeed of your horoscope.

Although all the information in this book is relevant and can construct an accurate astrological profile, you can go much, much further. It might surprise you to learn that there are other divisions of the zodiac, and indeed there are other zodiacs quite apart from the one with which we are all so familiar. There is, for instance, a system by which the sky is divided into 36 parts called decans and another based on the movements of the Moon. These are called the Lunar Mansions. And, as if this were not enough, every single one of the 360 degrees of the zodiac has its own individual interpretation, some of which are based on the meanings of stars far, far away from our own little, cozy family of planets.

As well as the major planets listed throughout this book, there are also the minor planets or asteroids such as Ceres, Juno, and Pallas that could be taken into account.

Without getting too complicated, the birth chart that you now have can be used in different ways. This book has been about character assessment based on your personal horoscope, but this eternally unchanging diagram that is unique to you can now be used to give indications of the future utilizing a variety of methods such as transits, progressions, arcs, and solar returns.

Of course, all this is well beyond the scope of this book, which set out to demonstrate that astrology can be easy when approached in an uncomplicated manner. If any of these more complex elements appeal to you, then many of the books listed in the bibliography will help you on your stellar journey. It's just one small step to continue your exploration of the wonderful world of astrology.

Bibliography

Understanding Astrology	Sasha Fenton	Thorsons 1991
Moon Signs	Sasha Fenton	Aquarian 1989
Rising Signs	Sasha Fenton	Aquarian 1989
Sun Signs	Sasha Fenton	Thorsons 1995
The Planets	Sasha Fenton	Thorsons 1994
The Hidden Zodiac	Sasha Fenton	Zambezi 2002
The Moon Sign Kit	Sasha Fenton & Jonathan Dee	Collins & Brown 2000
Moon Signs	Sybil Leek	Pan 1977
The Compleat Astrologer	Derek & Julia Parker	Mitchell Beazley 1971
Parker's Astrology	Derek and Julia Parker	Dorling Kindersley 1991
Future Now	Derek & Julia Parker	Mitchell Beazley 1988
Sun, Moon and Planet Signs	Lyn Birkbeck	Bloomsbury 1990
The Round Art	AT Mann	Paper Tiger 1979
Life Cycles	Rose Elliot	MacMillan 1993
Zodiac Signs	Frederick Goodman	Brian Todd 1990
The Only Astrology Book you'll Ever Need	Joanna Martine Woolfolk	Madison 2001
The House Book	Stephanie Camilleri	Llewelyn 1999
The Instant Astrologer	Felix Lyle & Bryan Aspland	Piatkus 1998

Picture credits

Star sign, sun, moon, and element illustrations by David Ashby

Photographs p 9 & 25 by Colin Bowling

Pictures pp 10, 21t, 22br, 25t, 30bl, 31, 32br, 33, 36, 37t, 39bl, 45b, 46, 47t, 49, 51b, 53, 56t, 56c(2) 67b, 73br, 68br, 74br, 75, 76t, 79br, 80tr, 82tr, 83br, 94br, 102tr, 103br, 116lc, 116br, 118, 119t, 121b, © Getty Images

Pictures pp 7, 13, 14, 15, 16, 17, 18, 19, 20, 21b, 22tr, 24, 34, 35, 37c, 37b, 38, 39tr, 40, 41, 42, 43, 44, 45t, 47b, 48, 50, 51t, 52, 55, 56c(1), 56b, 58, 63, 64, 65, 66, 67t, 68tr, 73bl, 73bc, 74tr, 74bl, 76b, 77, 78, 79tl, 80bl, 81, 82bl, 83tl, 90, 91, 92, 93, 94tl, 99, 100, 101, 102bl, 103tl, 104, 105, 108, 109, 110, 111, 112, 116tl, 117, 119b, 120, 121t, 122, © Stockbyte

(where b = bottom, t = top, l = left, c = center, r = right)